every grain of sand

A MEMOIR

David P. Wichman
with Heather Ebert

W. Brand Publishing
NASHVILLE, TENNESSEE

"David Wichman is a true original, a unique spirit. He combines openheartedness with erotic wisdom and a tender appreciation of the wounded, of the lonely, of all that's human in the most and least approachable of us. I will always be interested in what he has to report from that frontier where sex and spirit and loving-kindness merge."
—Patrick Mulcahey, television writer, *The Bold and the Beautiful*

"David Wichman truly understands the transformational cycle of trauma and recovery. His unique words of wisdom and heart-centered perspective are a force for good among everyone who encounters him. He has earned the love, respect, and admiration of so many other people who have struggled through the ups and downs of life. I wholeheartedly believe that *Every Grain of Sand* will have a memorable, wide-reaching impact."
—Sarah Prout, best-selling author, motivational speaker, founder of Manifesting Academy

"David Wichman's powerfully positive spirit permeates every room he enters. Having known him now for more than ten years, I can say *Every Grain of Sand* is a perfect title for his journey. Though unique, his words lend a healing perspective to all. I adore him as a person. I respect him as a being who found peaceful strength through his trials in life. Like a phoenix, he is an inspiration, and I'm so proud to call him my friend. Savor his words of wisdom with love in your heart."
—Debby Holiday, No. 1 Billboard dance recording artist and daughter of Jimmy Holiday

"Brutal and wonderful. It amazed me by revealing the number of emotions still unnamed."
—Bud Gundy, Emmy Award–winning producer and Lambda Literary Award finalist

"In knowing David Wichman, I've seen how his words, wisdom, and personality have been a force for good among everyone who encounters him. He has earned the love and respect of so many people who have struggled through trauma and recovery, and I'm confident that *Every Grain of Sand* will have a wide-reaching impact."
—Jason Goldberg, transformational speaker and internationally best-selling author of *Prison Break: Vanquish the Victim, Own Your Obstacles, and Lead Your Life*

"*Every Grain of Sand* is a brave and compelling memoir of recovery from the almost unimaginable abuse David Wichman experienced as a child and later inflicted on himself with alcoholism and drug addiction. It is not, however, a sad tale of victimization. Instead, David's essentially hopeful and resilient nature illuminates his story. His journey is ultimately a spiritual one told with honesty and conviction. He is also to be commended for writing frankly, positively, and unapologetically about his career as a sex worker and male companion. I've been telling him for years to write his story, and I'm glad he finally got around to it."
—Michael Nava, Lambda Literary Award winner of the *Henry Rios* novels

"No matter the circumstance, David's story demonstrates that love, compassion, and forgiveness encourage acceptance and healing."
—Mary Mazurek, GRAMMY-nominated recording engineer

"David Wichman's memoir grabbed me and wouldn't let me go. It blew my mind! Not only because of the events David survived as a child and his subsequent struggle to be free of the demons of his past, but that he writes with such clarity and honesty. His transformation is beyond miraculous. In the end, the book goes from memoir to self-help as we witness David's transformation from victim to guru, but without an ounce of self-importance. Only love, gratitude, and forgiveness."
—Nelsie Spencer, novelist and screenwriter

"Miracle. It's a word too often used in recovery circles. David's memoir, however, walks us through a life that can't be described in any other term. David shares the crucible of his life and walks readers through the alchemy of his transformation from base metal to gold. His life and his journey are nothing short of a miracle. My life is made better for having born witness to his. Thank you."
—Ralph Bruneau, PhD, psychotherapist, trauma and addiction specialist, International Mister Leather 2017

"This harrowing account of abuse and self-realization isn't another memoir played strictly for tragedy. It takes aim at your heart and then digs somewhere deeper, rustling our very souls. Wichman isn't simply interested in what it means to survive. He wants us to understand what it means to forgive. Along the way, he challenges everything you may believe about sex work, lifting it beyond the physical into something far more spiritual. You may never think of escorts the same way again."
—Mark S. King, award-winning writer, activist, five-time GLAAD Media Award nominee for *My Fabulous Disease*

"A powerful and thought-provoking story that everyone, no matter what their situation in life, can relate to. David takes the reader on a soul-searching journey of inner strength that one person can have to overcome adversity in their life. *Every Grain of Sand* will move you.
—Gary Saperstein, radio host, owner, Out In the Vineyard

"*Every Grain of Sand* is a heartbreaking memoir that I could not put down, a story of pain, of the search for one's place in the world, and of the transformative power of forgiveness. David Wichman has lived a thousand lives—some agonizing, some sublime—and we're lucky he survived them all with his talent and compassion intact."
—Dave Holmes, writer, producer, and television personality; editor-at-large, *Esquire*; author of *Party of One: A Memoir in 21 Songs*

"David Wichman's memoir is a provocative and heartfelt account of his journey to overcome personal struggles and demons to embrace his true nature as an educator and healer. Coming out of a challenging early life, his story aims to empower others in their efforts to conquer fear and shame so they can create a powerful and successful future. Although the journey is often painful and frustrating, Wichman reminds us that the process of self-acceptance and developing our life path is possible and that none of us are truly alone when we stop hurting ourselves and remain open to the opportunities around us."
—Brent Heinze, LPC, author of *Redefining Normal: A Modern Gay Man's Guide to Happy and Healthy Living*

Some names and places have been changed to protect individuals in the story.

j.brand@wbrandpub.com

W. Brand Publishing

www.wbrandpub.com

Cover design by JuLee Brand / designchik.net

Cover photo ©2019 by Jason deCaires Taylor

Every Grain of Sand/ David P. Wichman with Heather Ebert
—1st ed.

Available in Paperback, Kindle, and eBook formats.

Paperback ISBN: 978-1-950385-13-3

eBook ISBN: 978-1-950385-14-0

Library of Congress Control Number: 2019918180

contents

For Shari

For all who are experiencing the unimaginable,
For those requesting love in ways almost
no one understands,
For you in the midst of unspeakable injustice and
deafening silence,
You who feel alone, unloved, and unlovable,
You are my why.
What I know is this:
You will never be broken.
It's your light that shines brighter than most,
and that is why they see you.
That is why they are afraid.
For you have seen the true darkness.
There are many of us who are seeking you.
Your only job now is to light the way.
Shine, my love, shine, so they keep seeing you.
It's what you were born to do.

This book is for you.
Love, David

FOREWORD

Pema Chödrön, one of my favorite spiritual teachers, wrote, "To be fully alive, fully human, and completely awake is to be continually thrown out of the nest. To live fully is to be always in no-man's-land, to experience each moment as completely new and fresh. To live is to be willing to die over and over again."[1]

As David Wichman's story makes clear, he is someone who longs to be fully alive and completely awake. Since childhood, he has demonstrated a sensitivity to the ineffable, one that was tragically short-circuited by neglect and abuse from the adults in his life he believed he could trust. But our spirits—our essential selves—are not so easily daunted. From childhood abuse to surviving on the streets, to white-collar crime and embracing second chances, an undercurrent of hope pulses beneath his narrative, reminding us that all is never lost—at least not that which is most essential. No matter how many obstacles we may face, if we're willing to listen to our souls, we can always find our way back to our true purpose.

Like David, I too have been thrown out of the nest by grief and loss and wandered around no-man's-land, only to emerge transformed by the experience. As a result, we both share a passion for awakened living—engaging with ourselves and the world around us from a place of witness consciousness,

---

1 Pema Chödrön, When Things Fall Apart: Heart Advice for Difficult Times (Boulder: Shambhala Publications, 1996), 95.

rather than from our habitual, ingrained thought patterns. A person who has awakened to their true essence no longer sees the world in black and white, right and wrong, good and bad. An awakened person takes responsibility for their thoughts, words, and actions—for those are what create our life's experiences.

As I've gotten to know David through encounters in the recovery community and as his awakening coach, I can say without a doubt that he is one of the most enthusiastic and energetic people I know. Over the past few years, I've had the privilege of walking alongside him as he has explored inner obstacles and core beliefs that might have been keeping him from consciously creating the life he truly desired. He displays a rare courage to look deeply within himself, face his demons, and emerge with gems of wisdom for himself and others.

Though *Every Grain of Sand* is largely about David's recovery from severe drug addiction, I hope that anyone who reads it will recognize how all of us find ways to escape being fully present with ourselves and with *what is*—whether through alcohol or drugs, television, food, sex, shopping, social media, or any other adequate distraction from our thoughts and feelings. We all look outside ourselves for relief, and though not all coping strategies are as destructive as crystal meth, all such efforts take us away from the experience of our essential selves and the joy of being.

The good news is that no matter what has happened in our lives, beneath all of our behavior is a whole and perfect spiritual being—a revolutionary idea in a world in which we chronically perceive ourselves as broken or damaged in some way. We create our lives from these core beliefs and confirm their apparent truth by the resulting experiences. As this story illustrates, we can only break destructive patterns with love and compassion for ourselves and others.

David is someone who continues to do whatever it takes to heal so that he can be a beneficial presence on the planet. He has an unmistakable passion to share his message of love with as many people as possible. Anyone who encounters him will notice, in an instant, the passion he has for that deep calling.

Through his courage and willingness to share his journey authentically and transparently, David invites us all to look more deeply within ourselves and to trust that the transformation on the other side is completely worth any shadows we encounter along the way. I completely affirm his message, as it's my message as well: We are whole, perfect, and divine. Any assumptions of brokenness are an illusion we've bought into, and it's our life purpose to be liberated from such an illusion.

—T. J. Woodward

Best-selling author, inspirational speaker,
and revolutionary recovery specialist

AUTHOR'S NOTE

This memoir is an account of my life as I remember it to the best of my ability, given the nature of trauma and decades of severe alcoholism and drug addiction. Tracing the blurry timeline of events was difficult at best. Choosing what stayed in and what was left out was a heart-wrenching process. There are stories and details of great depth and weight that are sadly missing from the narrative. Some of the stops along the journey have been consolidated for the sake of brevity and thematic consistency.

Due to the intimate nature of my life's work, and for the safety and privacy of my clients and myself, many names and details have been changed or omitted. The underlying story and the mission of this book remains fully intact.

INTRODUCTION

The first time I ever took a hit of LSD was one of the most profound experiences of my life.

I was a sophomore at the time and living in a foster home with three other boys—all of us had been removed from abusive or otherwise untenable home environments. On this particular afternoon, I ingested a small square of gel I had picked up from a dealer at school and then hopped on a city transit bus on Mission Boulevard headed from Union City to Fremont, the city where I'd grown up.

A good hour later, just as the acid trip started to peak, I found myself back in my old neighborhood. I descended the bus steps and started walking. I rounded a corner to see the red-lettered Exxon sign above the gas station where I had sold candy bars for Little League to drivers lined up during the gas shortages years earlier. I strolled past an old friend's house where broken-down cars were perched on cinder blocks in the front yard. And then I found myself standing across from my own family's ranch-style house—my former place of imprisonment, the setting of my stepfather's merciless abuse, the environment in which my spirit was tormented and broken until the day I escaped to the safety of foster care.

On any other day, the sight of this place would have filled me with rage and longing and the sheer agony of remembrance. But my acid trip had escorted me into a new dimension. My mind had opened to an experience of unending love and total forgiveness for everyone and everything that had ever harmed me. This love permeated the air; I walked in bliss. I felt as if a conscious being accompanied me, perhaps Jesus himself or what some call Christ Consciousness—a higher self that understands we are all connected and one with a universal force of love. In this sacred state of awakening, I could see forgiveness clearly, and I fully comprehended that every human being—no matter what they've done to others or themselves—is redeemable.

The idea that my stepfather could be forgiven for his cruelty overwhelmed me with relief. Even as I basked in benevolence and loving-kindness, I couldn't grasp the concept that any one of my abusers could coexist alongside humanity in this enlightened space—and yet there in my core I found absolute compassion. Beyond mere forgiveness, this feeling was one of pure love and the acceptance of that same love in everyone. I lost all sense of self—I was part of everyone and everything, a cohesive organism, a fantastic tapestry of incredible, overwhelming existence.

My brain opened up to this well of conscious awareness, and my soul sensed this deep, undeniable truth. The hours spent in this heightened state of being awakened an inner knowing, one as ancient as the cosmos. The world so filled with war, suffering, and division didn't seem ready for this profound message, and I certainly didn't feel worthy of spreading it. So, the belief descended into the deepest recesses of my being, and as this enlightened, colorful state faded, my brokenness reemerged, the skies perpetually overcast.

I took LSD many more times—some trips were cosmic and others hellish—but no chemical substance ever opened me again to that same divine, all-encompassing, unchangeable love. And I believe most of my drug use in the years afterward—every drag on a joint, every snort of cocaine, every injection of crystal meth—was simply an attempt to get back to that place of higher consciousness. After some time, my drug use devolved into an ongoing mission to blot out the pain of not being able to find that freedom again and to escape living with the brokenness that I thought defined me.

Over the years following that peak experience, I descended into the deepest pits of helplessness and despair. I aged out of foster care and ended up homeless on the streets of San Francisco, not a penny to my name, no skills or education, no one to pull me up out of the gutter. I turned to sex work to survive. Outside the safety of a traditional family unit, I found my support in transgender street workers, gay hustlers on Polk Street, drug dealers, hookers, and misfits of all kinds.

I sought refuge in shelters such as the United States Mission and stood in food lines at Glide Church and Saint Anthony's. Most of the people who fed me or gave me a place to sleep are now dead and gone, but they live on in my memory as family. Sometimes I found temporary jobs filing papers, answering phones, or sweeping floors, after which I returned to the shabby and squalid Delta Hotel on Sixth Street, San Francisco's Skid Row. Many of these circumstances were of my own making; I was doing the best I could with the knowledge and maturity I had at the time.

My life pivoted sharply in September 2005, and after decades of struggle and failure, I found my way to freedom from my addictions, as well as an abiding gratitude for the wonder of my own existence. My spiritual journey revealed within me a state of grace—an inner peace and gratitude for each moment. The spiritual experience I longed for never needed to be "found" in the first place—I was already living it, but completely unaware.

My mentor and life coach, T. J. Woodward, reminds me to ask what else is possible. He says, "What if these years of destruction, drinking, and using drugs were a brilliant strategy that just finally stopped working?" He notes that our younger selves, who were brilliant thinkers fighting to survive in the midst of trauma, found ways to endure unspeakable pain. As adults, we continue to use something outside of ourselves to fix something that feels broken within. The pain of unresolved trauma and my belief in my inherent brokenness often blocked my ability to be in the present moment and find joy. It's hard to imagine that a loaded syringe was a brilliant strategy, but the more I discover about myself, the more I see how true that was.

Some people addicted to drugs or alcohol use those substances to seek oblivion and escape from their inner pain. I find it interesting that the solution to many addictions prescribed by 12-step programs is a "fundamental spiritual change." In other words, a spiritual awakening. I believe that all of us, on some level, are seeking a connection to something beautiful and whole, and at some point or another, we will wake up to the truth of who we are. When we do, we will see this pure, priceless, immeasurable beauty, which is our truth.

The recognition may come and go. We may transform, shift, and expand, but the truth is always there. Our true identity, our innermost being, has been covered up by what our teachers, parents, peers, society, and religions have taught us for years. Many of us find out that this is the road to unlearning the illusions. The path to healing or the journey to enlightenment is not the gaining of new, more profound, deeper information about our soul's purpose, but the discovery of what has been there all along.

My story is not merely about addiction or for people suffering from addiction—it's for anyone trapped in loneliness and limiting beliefs about their worthiness. This story is also meant to illuminate and eliminate the shame and self-loathing that plagues communities across all demographics, borders, and socioeconomic lines. It's about liberating our minds and hearts to give and receive love. We all need true freedom from shame—especially the self-destructive and often deadly shame of our complex sexual experiences, traumas, and desires.

This story is not happening to me any longer; it's happening *through* me. I stand with it and carry it as my light. I believe we are all messengers, and we have come to share a message that brings us closer to love and closer to kindness as a way of life, where kindness becomes our first response instead of a reaction born of fear and self-protection. When our fears drive our actions, we pay dearly, passing on our toxicity and negative memories, our collective shame and learned behaviors, from generation to generation. The world is awakening to this realization. The shift has begun. I believe the essence of every individual is an immeasurable wealth of love and wholeness. It's the truth of who we are. Our worst traumas neither destroy us nor define us. As we wake up from the brokenness and begin to live from this incorruptible place of being, we heal. We begin to live out our dreams and our purpose on this planet. We finally find an empowering sense of peace.

My hope is that anyone who reads this book might find liberation from the illusions of brokenness. We don't always have to forgive the unforgivable or attain some unreachable ideal of empowerment, but we can come to a place of deep compassion and understanding for what happened around us during our storm—our traumas—and move it through us and out of us. We don't have to claim it any longer as our staff of righteous survival. I encourage those of you who have awakened and emerged from your own darkness to continue to carry your message by being just who you are right now. Keep shining your light so others can find their way home.

CHAPTER 1

SEPTEMBER 20, 2005

I swung my legs out from under the thin cotton blanket and rested my feet on the cold concrete floor. In the early morning, my cellblock remained still and dark. Despite the weariness permeating my bones, I'd barely slept at all.

This was it—Judgment Day.

The Santa Rita Jail in Dublin, California, had confined me for the past nine months, but by the end of the day, I would know whether I was leaving jail at last or doomed to a federal prison for decades to come.

I stood up slowly and pulled out my prison uniform. For appearance in federal court, I had the right to dress in normal clothing, but whatever normal clothes I was wearing the day of my arrest had gotten lost inside the county system, so I had no civilian clothes at all. The best I could do was a clean, ironed, white T-shirt that José, one of the jail trustees, had secured for me from the laundry, a pair of red scrub pants, and shower shoes I'd been given during intake.

Santa Rita Jail in Alameda County is an enormous facility that houses more than four thousand inmates—typically convicted felons sentenced to county jail or those still awaiting arraignment, trial, or sentencing. The men in our maximum-security pod were under protective custody and segregated from the general population. Our group of inmates included informants, gays, transgendered women, and horny straight guys who wanted an easier stay—all rather harmless people at risk of being killed or maimed by the violent felons and gang lords on the other side.

Our pod also kept federal holds—guys like me facing prison time for federal crimes. My list of charges included possession of controlled substances, conspiracy to commit credit card fraud, fraud and related activity, possession of stolen mail, and possession of stolen identities—all of it the racket my then-boyfriend, Richard, and I had used to fund our relentless drug habit. Addiction owned me then, mind, body, and spirit. I wholly and completely belonged to the oblivion. As a result, I'd spent nearly a year in this hellhole with the possibility of many more to come.

Cleaned up and dressed, I sat tensely on the edge of the metal bunk bed, my hands clasped and my gaze down, when the cell door buzzed. The sound jolted me like a bolt of electricity. The next thing I heard was the deputy calling my name. It was time to go.

The deputies entered my cell to cuff my wrists and shackle my ankles for the transport to the federal courthouse in San Francisco. Hindered by the restraints, I could only shuffle between two guards out of my cell and through the ward. The cellblock had begun to come to life, but the other inmates, still drowsy from sleep and knowing where I was headed, spoke few words, mostly just offering a nod or a look that meant good luck. Tamica, one of the transgender women, yelled out, "Miss David!" I usually hated being called that, but she said it with love, and I needed to hear it that morning. "You gonna be fine—don't worry," she said, waving.

Outside, the transport unit—a motor coach with different sections of interior caging—stood ready to receive the line of us en route to court. The guards placed me in a seat within the locked cage for prisoners in protective custody before unshackling my arms and legs. I rubbed my wrists and stared through the tinted windows, seeing nothing. I thought back to earlier conversations with my defense attorney, Nina Wilder.

When I last saw her, Nina had asked me to be patient while the prosecution built their case. For much of my time in Santa Rita, I'd had little communication from Nina or anyone in the court system—no dates, no guidance, no news from the outside world. I had written letter after letter to the court asking for even one iota of a clue as to what to expect. It wasn't until August that I finally had my plea arraignment, in which I agreed to plead guilty to one charge so the prosecution would drop the rest. But the morning of my sentencing, I had no idea what to expect. The stress of not knowing made me crazy.

On the bus across from me sat another federal prisoner, a handsome, muscular black man named Marius who had been busted with ten grams of speed. He too was headed for a sentencing hearing, but unlike me, he remained calm and at ease.

"Yeah, my baby mama gonna hit me up with some cash on the books, and I'll do my thirty-six months and be outta there," he bragged.

I didn't know how many baby mamas he had, but even in his yellow jailhouse clothes, he was so sexy he could have had any baby mama he wanted.

Given the sentencing guidelines for drug possession with intent to distribute methamphetamines, Marius was looking at three to ten years. He had a girlfriend and a baby and a life on the outside, so he trusted he would get a lenient sentence. I wished I shared his confidence. Maximum sentences on the combined total of my charges added up to fifty-five years, though my plea deal reduced the probable jail time to something between three and ten years like Marius's case. I could barely tolerate the thought of even one more day in that jail, let alone a decade.

After the forty-mile ride into the city, our transport unit pulled into a parking garage beneath the Phillip Burton Federal Building and United States Courthouse. The monolithic concrete and glass structure runs the length of a city block on Golden Gate Avenue in the heart of San Francisco's Civic Center. One by one, we submitted our hands and feet back into the shackles and descended from the bus.

Fear coursed through my veins and rattled my bones. I felt weak, and the weight of exhaustion bore down on my whole body. I found myself in almost constant prayer to a god I barely believed in. Beyond a miracle, what hope did I have left? The only thing that consoled me was knowing one way or another, the waiting would be over. After such a long, harsh battle, the closure would bring a measure of relief, even as I dreaded the possibility of being locked indefinitely in a human cage.

A team of deputies led us through a system of tunnels, hallways, and secure elevators until we arrived at a large holding area on an upper floor of the courthouse. I waited there until my name was called, and then a guard escorted me down to a smaller holding cell outside of my judge's courtroom. The cement cell had no windows—just an entry door and a side door that led to a glass conference room where inmates could meet with their attorneys in advance of their hearings.

In my holding cell sat four other guys, including Marius, all of us slouched on cold metal benches bolted to the wall. I stared at the floor, trying to piece together the years of my life and series of decisions that had led me to this place. I shook my head in disbelief that this was what I had become. If only I could start over again, do a few things differently—but it felt useless to hope or dream. The flood of stress and confusion overwhelmed me. I kept my thoughts centered on whatever I could. I needed to keep my wits about me—today was no day to fall apart.

When Marius's case got called, I straightened up a bit and nodded at him. He smiled and gave a thumbs-up before following the bailiff out of the cell.

I wondered how he would fare in his hearing. This was no county courthouse. This was a federal institution where everyone dressed in their Sunday best on a daily basis to appear before the judge. And this was no low-level magistrate either. Inside the courtroom presided a stern district judge named Phyllis J. Hamilton who had been appointed by President Bill Clinton and made famous for her controversial decision to strike down the Partial Birth Abortion Ban Act earlier that year. She followed the rules. Her court went by the book. That's just how it was.

While I waited, Nina appeared at the glass side door; she was a small but fierce Jewish woman who spoke straight and sharp. I exhaled loudly when I saw her. She motioned for me to join her in the conference room next to the holding cell.

"David, you have to stop writing letters to the court! You're not helping your case," she said, straightening a stack of papers on the table. After a brief reminder of the plea deal she'd worked out with the prosecutors, she continued, "Listen, I have no idea what's going to happen. This could go in any direction. We don't even know what kind of mood the judge is in today. Just don't expect any mercy. And don't you dare go in there and talk about how you found God."

After a bit of coaching on what I should say to Judge Hamilton, Nina released me, and I returned to my spot in the holding cell. I was staring at the ceiling, rehearsing my prepared speech, when Marius returned from his hearing.

The moment he entered the cell, the outcome was evident; his face revealed his devastation. He rushed to the corner, fell to his knees before the toilet, and threw up. When he finished, he slouched against the wall, exhausted and nearly catatonic. He'd gotten eight years, nearly a year for every gram he'd had in his possession, and he would have to serve 85 percent of that time, no matter what. The federal system had no good-behavior program, and though there were ways to get a sentence reduced or be granted an exception, such motions were extremely rare.

Marius shook his head slowly back and forth. The justice system isn't kind to people of color, especially black men, who are routinely sentenced more harshly than any other demographic—a horrid fact of our system. For Marius, this fact was his new reality. We chatted a bit, making small talk to distract him from the world crashing down around him. He was still recovering from the blow when a deputy buzzed the door to take him back upstairs.

After his sentencing, I could barely breathe. He had been so confident he wouldn't get sentenced harshly, but he did. I couldn't conceive of spending eight years on the inside. I wasn't confident at all about my chances before this judge. Even as a white man without an extensive criminal record, I couldn't predict what would happen in the federal system. No one, not even my attorney, had been able to discern what would happen in my case. The judge might be lenient and give me the lesser sentence, or she might decide to make an example of me to deter other white-collar criminals. After what she had handed to this guy, my last ounce of hope dissipated altogether. I was fully convinced she was going to send me away.

My case wasn't called until late in the day. When the door clicked and the bailiff finally said my name, I nearly jumped out of my skin. This was it. I took a deep breath and stood up to go. No matter what happened in the next few minutes, I knew only one thing for sure—my life was never, ever going to be the same again.

CHAPTER 2

When I was little, our family lived on Argonaut Street in Stockton, California. My mom, Linda, and dad, Gary, had had two kids ahead of me—my brother, Donnie, three years older, and my sister, Shari, a year older. My parents divorced when I was around two years old. My dad had gotten another woman pregnant at the same time as my mom became pregnant with me. Two new sons later, the choice between families was made on his behalf; he was also an alcoholic, and after a violent fight, my mom kicked him out. He went on to marry the other woman—a heavy-set, Pall Mall–smoking, loving woman named Ginger who owned an adult bookstore called Gin's Books. As bizarre as the scenario sounds, little did I know that my dad's household would end up being the one so full of love.

By the time I was three and my older brother was starting school, my mom had also remarried. My stepfather, Jim, was a handsome man who sported a beard and mustache and drove both a Triumph Chopper and a Dodge Charger. He reminded me of Burt Reynolds. Jim worked as a cartographer for the United States Geological Survey in Menlo Park, monitoring seismic activity, surveying natural disasters, and drawing maps, which I always thought was a cool job. My mother was a stunningly beautiful woman who worked full time as a CPA while I was growing up, first for a bank and later for large companies, including one that made daisy wheels for printers.

My mom and Jim packed up and moved us to Fremont, about sixty-five miles east of Stockton and the fourth largest city in the San Francisco Bay Area. Long before Fremont became the new tech-industry hub of the Bay Area, peppered with McMansions and BMWs, I remember open, rolling fields and horse stables on the hillsides, middle-income tract housing, and cul-de-sacs lined with modest ranch houses of similar layout and design.

When I was just starting school, I would ride my bike all over the area alongside other little rug rats in our neighborhood until the streetlights came on, our signal that we were due home for dinner. My friends and I often snuck into the local pickle factory and jumped into barrels to dig out cucumbers. We had to get out of the barrels and pedal fast away before the factory guards started shooting us with rock salt. For several years of my early childhood, I rode like the wind on my black and silver Huffy bicycle, enjoying the unique freedom that belongs to that age of innocence.

In the beginning of this new life with Mom and Jim, there was kindness. Before his attempts at love gave way to cruelty, there were tender moments that stand out in my recollection like question marks, asking how and why things could have disintegrated so fully afterward.

One such moment happened in kindergarten, the day of our class Halloween parade—only I had no idea a party awaited me that day at school. When I walked into a classroom full of kids dressed as Superman, Wonder Woman, ghosts, goblins, and witches, I withered beneath the heat of humiliation. There I stood, a skinny little kid in Sears toughskin jeans, a yellow T-shirt that made me look like Charlie Brown, a Levi's jean jacket, and Hush Puppies waffle stomper boots. Despite wearing my favorite clothes, I was the only kid without a costume and felt entirely left out.

A teacher took pity on me. She pulled out a wide-brimmed hat like something a society lady would wear and placed it on my head. When the kids laughed at this fancy "costume," I turned beet red and wanted nothing more than to escape. My family lived only four blocks from the school, so when the parade commenced, I ditched the lame hat and bolted toward home to hide.

When I burst through the front door, my stepfather was cooking oatmeal. He looked up and immediately knew from the look on my face that something was wrong.

"Why aren't you at school?" he asked, tuned into my inner experience, perhaps for the only time in my life, then or since.

I shoved my hands deep into my pockets and stared at the floor. I made some excuse, like "some dumb party" or "it's not really school today."

Just then, the procession of dressed-up school kids clamored past the house, and an expression of knowing came over Jim's face. This strange new man in my life recognized I had no costume.

He dashed to his bedroom and reemerged with one of his flannel shirts, a garment big enough to lose me in. He ran out to the garage and returned with a couple of old pillows and a rope. Pulling my mother's kitchen shears from a drawer, he cut down the sleeves, stuffed my belly with the pillows, and tied the rope around the bottom to hold it all together. He looked me over with a quizzical look, as if something were missing. He nodded and went back to the bedroom, returning with my mother's brown eyeliner—a mortal sin if ever there was one—which he used to draw a stubbly beard on my small face. He stuffed his white Navy sailor cap with newspaper and perched it on my head, and then to top it all off, he dug out his smallest fishing rod. He filled a red bandana with pillow stuffing and tied it to the end of the rod.

His creation was complete—he had dressed me as a hobo, a bum. Before sending me out to catch up with the parade, he bent down, rubbed his prickly whiskers on my face, and said, "Everything's going to be all right."

And, at least for that moment, it was. I felt cared for, I felt loved, and I truly believed everything would be okay. In hindsight, it's telling that I was being dressed as a hobo by a man who would soon find it hard to even look at me, let alone love and accept me. But at the time, he could have dressed me as a cockroach, and I would have been thrilled.

I hoisted my fishing rod above my head and ran to join the parade. Joy and pride in my homemade costume carried me like a pair of wings. I was a son with a new dad. I was a kid who belonged. I fit in; I neither stood out nor disappeared among my classmates, even if just for one day.

One Easter, *The Greatest Story Ever Told* aired on television in all its Charlton Heston glory. I loved that movie, even though I had no religious upbringing. My mother had attended a Catholic high school and college, and my stepfather didn't smoke and only drank wine, but neither of them was a practicing Catholic.

Stored in the garage among my stepdad's *National Geographic* magazines was an old Bible he never read, but when he noticed my fascination with the television drama about Jesus of Nazareth, he gave me his Bible as an Easter gift—the first present I ever received from him. My new Bible had a dusty black cover made of textured, bonded leather with a copper-colored zipper around the outside. On the front in gold inlay lettering, *The Holy Bible, King James Version*. Jim had signed an interior page along with the date of his gift. I traced his signature with my fingers and then flipped through the pages to look at colored illustrations of biblical events—Adam and Eve, Noah's ark, David and Goliath, Jesus and his twelve disciples.

I went through a definitive Jesus phase as a child, which began one afternoon when a Jehovah's Witness appeared on our front porch. When I opened the door, I looked up at her, curious and unreserved.

"Hello," she said, smiling. She bent down and stuck in front of my face a Polaroid picture of Jesus in the clouds. Given how much I had explored my illustrated Bible, I recognized this picture as a storybook image of Jesus's ascension to the heavens.

But she had a more interesting story: "My friend Esmeralda was on a flight coming home from Los Angeles, and she took this picture from the window of the airplane." The woman shook the Polaroid picture as if it wasn't yet fully developed. "Look at what she saw—this is proof that Jesus is coming back!"

My eyes widened. It makes me laugh in hindsight, but in the moment, I was enthralled. "What! Jesus is coming back?" I felt an insane amount of excitement, followed by deflated disbelief. *Surely this can't be true.*

Naturally, the witnessing woman invited me to her church, and I begged my mom to take me. She indulged my curiosity, and the next thing I remember is all kinds of awkwardness inside a Kingdom Hall. At the rear stood a man playing a harmonica louder than the instrument was ever designed to be played, while people streamed to the altar to have elders pray over them. Everything about this place struck me as strange and uncomfortable, and I couldn't wait to go home.

After that, my mom decided it would be a good idea to send me to a Catholic Mass. Down the street from our house was a Spanish Mission–style Catholic parish called Santa Paula. Although she didn't accompany us, Mom encouraged Donnie, Shari, and me to attend one Sunday morning. I got all dolled up in dark pants, a white button-down shirt, a tie, and shiny black shoes—the whole nine yards. I will never forget for as long as I live how beautiful and amazing this simple parish seemed to me. When we walked in, I thought, *Now, this is where Jesus is.*

An acoustic band played music at the front of the cathedral; the worship leader sang joyful songs. Despite the modern guitar, this was still a Catholic church with all the requisite pomp and circumstance—the procession of officiates, a swinging censer and smoky incense, the mystery of the Eucharist. From our seats on the wooden pew, I admired the handsome, charismatic priest, enthralled by his sermon. My siblings, less enthused, took off and went home.

Not only did I stay for the entire Mass, I stayed for the next service as well, which was a replica of the first, except in Spanish. Afterward, I rushed home and made a declaration to my amused mother: "When I grow up, I'm going to be a priest." And that was it. That's what I wanted to do.

My parents indulged my priestly ambitions and enrolled Shari and me in catechism classes so we could learn the tenets of the faith. The nuns at the parish told stories, taught lessons, and asked us questions whose answers we had to recite aloud: "Who created you?" "God did." "What else did God create?" "The whole universe." "Why did God create all these things?" "For His glory." The best part were chocolate cupcakes with chocolate frosting baked inside of ice cream cones, one of the most decadent treats I'd ever had.

The beauty and mystery of something as sublime as pure faith is never so accessible as it is to a childlike mind. As it goes, however, there comes a time when such innocence is lost. Or, in my case, abruptly stolen.

When I was six, I had very few friends at school. I tended to be the one who got picked on, the one nobody wanted to hang out with, the class wimp. In my neighborhood, however, I had a friend named Eddie McDonald who convinced me to do crazy things for extra money, like singing Christmas carols door to door. We knew "Jingle Bells," "Joy to the World" (but only the best parts), and all of "Santa Claus Is Coming to Town." At the end of a song, we held out an empty Play-Doh cup that adoring neighbor women filled with spare change. By the time we'd made the rounds, I went home with a sock full of coins.

In other seasons, we raked lawns. Eddie's ingenious plan: "Never give them a real price—just look real cute and ask for a tip." We were each scrawny and missing our front teeth. I can only imagine neighbors on our block laughed at us. Why not give these little guys some money? Who would have thought such young kids would have so much initiative? We probably never finished mowing or raking a single lawn, but we always managed to earn enough for a stash of candy.

One sunny afternoon, Eddie led me to a less benevolent benefactor.

"I know this guy—he lives up the street and has Pong. Wanna go play?" he asked.

"What's Pong?"

"It's this Atari game. C'mon, I'll have to show you."

Eddie and I walked a few blocks until we came upon three houses in a wide, open field. In the middle stood a lovely white Victorian that housed a local Baptist pastor and his family. A bit farther away to the right was a yellow house where an elderly couple lived. And directly to the left awaited our destination, a creepy two-story building painted a drab olive green with a large, empty downstairs that might have been a meeting hall for the Veterans of Foreign Wars or a Boy Scout troop.

At the front door, Eddie rang the bell, and we heard footsteps descending a staircase. A thirty-something man with a pasty white face and red hair appeared and motioned for us to follow him upstairs. His name was Norman, which was fitting, given that he was a total creep and lived in a house that looked like the Bates Motel.

I later learned that Norman worked in parts distribution for Peterbilt Motors and sang in the choir at the Baptist church across the field. This bachelor pad of sorts had small rooms and spaces set apart from each other by beaded curtains. Eddie made a beeline for the television set and game console and settled onto the floor with the handset to the Atari Pong, one of the first consumer video games on the market. I sat down on a pillow on the floor next to Eddie and watched with fascination as he lobbed what looked like a white digital cube from one side of the screen to the other.

Norman interrupted my fixation on the game.

"Wanna see something cool?" He turned on a palm-sized handheld massage device and pressed it against my legs. I relaxed into the pleasure of the vibration. Then, he slowly moved the device up to my crotch and stimulated my genitals.

At six years old, I experienced sexual arousal for the first time in my life.

Norman stood up and walked toward his bedroom. "Why don't you come in here, and I'll show you something *really* cool."

Confused and intrigued by these emerging feelings, I stood up and followed him. Eddie continued to play Pong, pretending not to notice. In the bedroom, Norman pulled down both our pants and started playing with me. The sexual acts are a blur, but I remember being mesmerized by the size of his penis and the force of his ejaculation. Such a bizarre sight enthralled me, and I wanted to see it over and over again. I reacted to the entire experience in childlike wonder: *This is fun! This is cool! This feels really good. And look what his thing does!*

When our odd tryst came to an end, we returned to the couch outside the television area. Eddie got up from his game and came over to where we sat.

"We gotta go," he said, looking at me. Then, he climbed onto Norman's lap and whispered into his ear, "You got a spare?"

Norman rose from the couch and reached on top of the refrigerator for a tray of change. He held it out while Eddie grabbed a handful of coins and stuffed them into his jeans pocket. Norman let me take some too, and then he held the door as we skipped back down the stairs.

Some part of me sensed what happened wasn't okay, but the thrill of it overrode the impression of wrongness. All I knew was that we could come over, play games, do fun and crazy things, and get money at the end. I returned to Norman's house a half dozen more times, spending ten to fifteen minutes there before I had to be home from school. I never told anyone about those visits, sensing the secrecy without knowing why. But then one day I arrived at his house to find him in tears.

Norman stood bent over in his kitchen, both hands resting on the table on either side of an open Bible. When he looked up at me, his eyes were red and watery, and his chest heaved from sobbing. He began reading passages of scripture.

"If a man also lie with mankind, as he lieth with a woman, both of them have committed an abomination: they shall surely be put to death; their blood shall be upon them." He flipped hunks of pages until he arrived at another passage. "Who knowing the judgment of God, that they which commit such things are worthy of death, not only do the same, but have pleasure in them that do them."

I struggled to make sense of this strange and scary language.

"These are the words of God, David," said Norman. "These verses describe what's going to happen to us. Everything we've been doing is wrong, and we're going to go to hell."

As the gravity of his words sunk in, panic overtook me, and I felt deep shame. I retreated inward until Norman sounded distant and far away. He described scenes of eternal hellfire and unending torment, as if each fingernail from my small hands would get ripped out over and over again. I shook my head to rid myself of these visions. I thought about the Bible my stepfather had given me, the holy grail of my possessions; everything in it must be true, including what Norman had just read aloud.

"We can never be together like this again, or I will go to prison," he said. "You can never come back here, and every night before you go to bed, you better beg God to forgive you for your sins."

I stared at the floor. Norman took my hand and led me into the living room.

"Get down on your knees and ask Jesus to forgive you," he said.

With his Bible in hand, he knelt down and began to pray words I don't remember. Shrouded in sheer awkwardness and horror, I felt the last vestiges of childhood disintegrate completely.

I turned to leave. Every step I took descending the staircase from Norman's apartment weighed me down with despair, shame, and guilt. I had been certain I was going to heaven. I had loved the Santa Paula parish. I had dreamed of becoming a priest. But then Norman said we had committed this mortal sin that surely doomed us to hell.

When I emerged from the house into that wide, grassy field, I watched the afternoon sunlight fade away. My fate sealed, I lost all hope. I remember every day after this moment as perpetually overcast. From that point onward, all other memories of my childhood are tinted gray and play out beneath a dreary, hazy sky.

The catechism classes changed from a fun after-school activity to a constant reminder of my appalling shame. At the end of the lessons, my entire family—Mom, Jim, Donnie, Grandpa Willy, and Aunt Jana—came to watch Shari and me take our first Holy Communion, a tortuous event. At the crux of the ceremony, young communicants lined up to meet with a priest on the dais at the front of the church. We were to confess a sin so he could offer us a prayer of absolution. I could never tell this priest what I had done with Norman. I didn't want him to know what a horrible child I was, and nothing else seemed like a sin in comparison.

When my turn came, this kind priest bent forward to receive my confession.

Unable to think of anything, I simply stated, "I am without sin."

He laughed and straightened up. Patting me on the head, he said, "You're cute. Don't worry, you'll sin soon enough."

On the short drive home, my stepfather looked at me in the rearview mirror. "Did you tell the priest what you did?"

Shame washed over me anew—did Jim know what I had done? I hadn't told a soul and wouldn't until nearly twenty years later. I assumed it was all my fault—I had gone looking for it, hadn't I? Surely Jim must have meant something else I had done wrong, but I couldn't think of what it was.

After that, it seemed I couldn't do anything right at all. The farther away from the parish we drove, the farther I felt from my aspirations to become a priest. Too tarnished and ruined for such a high calling, that holy and precious idea was quickly stomped out.

CHAPTER 3

The secret I shared with Norman I kept so closely guarded that it only emerged while I slept. At that age, I might have wet the bed occasionally, but it soon became much worse. Night after night, I soaked the sheets. Ashamed and embarrassed, I hid my wet pajamas and underwear and the dirty linens, crumpling them away in corners of my bedroom or stuffing them under the mattress to conceal the crime.

I thought both of my secrets were safe until a defining incident occurred that permanently altered my place in the family.

One afternoon, my parents were driving me home from my grandparents' house. If my siblings were in the car, I don't remember them. What I do remember is that my mother said, "David, we have something to show you when we get home." They looked knowingly at each other, maybe even amused, a vague smirk on each of their faces.

My parents had done something nice, just for me—or so I thought. I expected to come home to a sweet surprise, perhaps a special gift from the local catalog delivery service, the Jewel Tea Company. When we pulled into the driveway, I eagerly climbed out of the car and waited in anticipation as Jim unlocked the front door. We wandered through the entryway, dropping our things here and there, while I looked around for my surprise.

"Come in here," called Jim.

I walked into the living room where he and my mom waited by the coffee table. On the table was a brown paper bag. I knew immediately what was in it.

My stepfather flicked his fingers against the crinkled brown paper. "Open it!" he snarled. "Take out each pair. We're going to count them together. For each one, you're going to get the belt."

I felt the searing flush of humiliation, far beyond despair and abandonment. Frustrated by how slowly I was removing each pair of dirty underwear, Jim grabbed the paper bag and shoved it into my chest. I followed him to the garage where he made me put my dirty clothes into the washing machine.

"Pull down your pants," he said.

I was in shock, already terrified. When I pulled down my pants, Jim saw that I had soiled myself. Disgusted, he whipped me right then and there, as hard as he could swing. The sting and pain seethed through me. Hell became very real, and in this blur of insanity, I was convinced God himself was punishing me.

For each urine-soaked piece of clothing I added to the washer, Jim doled out a hard spanking with his belt. For one pair of underwear, *whack*! For the pajama bottoms, *whack*! For the matching top, *whack*! Though corporal punishment wasn't uncommon in that era, he took it to a whole other level. Worse than the pain of being lashed across my seat and the backs of my legs was the suffocating sense of betrayal. I was mortified, enraged, overcome with despair. I had been tricked into thinking something good was going to happen but then beaten instead. For as long as I live, I will never understand how my parents could have cheated me so viciously.

"Look at you," said my mother with a laugh. "You're turning six shades of red. You're going to kill yourself if you keep holding your breath like that."

She had abandoned me to Jim's abuse. Perhaps she didn't want to argue with him about whether it was right or wrong to raise kids this way. Even worse, perhaps she thought he was right. They were a team, united at the hip, and she had apparently decided to cosign his shit. The two of them volleyed turns at insane parenting.

"Stand still and shut up!" Jim yelled. "You're going to have to find a way to stop shitting your pants. What the fuck is wrong with you?"

"Why, David, would you wet your bed at your age? When will you grow up?" Mom said, still laughing.

Jim changed his tone. In a cunning and manipulative voice, he said, "From now on, all you have to do is tell us when you wet the bed, and we'll take care of it."

He handed the final toss back to my mother.

"Look at you," she said. "I can't stand the sight of you. Get out of here!"

Jim lashed my bare bottom one last time and sent me to bed, screaming for help.

Even more than being molested, this moment was one of the darkest marks on my life. Though my stepfather went on to make beating me his regular pastime, nothing he did afterward ever broke me as thoroughly as this sadistic, premeditated punishment. These two people I trusted appeared to be so disgusted that I was no longer worthy of love. In that moment, my spirit departed my body, and what was left was a ghost in the shape of a six-year-old boy. I'd been hollowed out by humiliation, excavated of any last sense of love and belonging.

From that point onward, I wanted to crawl out of my skin, escape the confines of my body, be anyone but me and anywhere but where I was. Despite knowing the consequences, I acted out repeatedly. I broke things around the house. I got near-failing grades in school. I stole money from my parents' dresser to buy candy. When I was older, I stole cigarettes from my mother's purse. The ramifications of misbehaving were so cruel it makes me wonder why I dared even breathe wrong as a child. Deep inside, some part of me decided I deserved punishment; perhaps if I endured enough hell now, I could avoid the actual fires of hell later, the eternal judgment Norman had warned me about.

Despite the harsh punishment—or perhaps because of it—the bed-wetting continued. Jim wouldn't let me change the sheets; he figured that if I had to sleep in my own piss, I would finally stop messing the bed. I remember how horrible it felt to come home from school and crawl into bed, a brownish yellow ring running around the center of the still-damp sheets. I sought relief by folding the dry areas into layers or throwing a towel or a T-shirt over the wet spot. My parents only allowed me to change the bed and wash my clothes once the smell became too overpowering or my brother, who shared my room, complained about the filth.

Besides regular whippings, my stepfather sentenced me to near-constant incarceration. From the time I was six until I was about twelve, my parents kept me locked up in my bedroom, only allowing me out for dinner or to do chores. My only outside excursions were to Little League games, perhaps to maintain the appearance of a happy family. I was so broken by then, however, that I was the worst player on the baseball team. When I was ten, I joined the Boy Scouts—Jim's attempt to teach us to be boys. I hated both Little League and the Boy

Scouts, but the games and meetings meant a modicum of freedom from constant lockdown.

When my stepfather wanted to increase the level of restriction, he ordered me not to move from my bed. If he walked in to find me in some other part of my room, the restriction was extended—not just for a couple of weeks but for months at a time and always accompanied by a beating. My bedroom door had no lock, so whenever my parents left the house, Jim ran Scotch tape across the knob and along the doorframe to keep me contained. I'd escaped so many times that now he thought he had me. If I broke the seal along the door, they would know I'd gotten out.

When I was only seven, I decided to run away. I packed a few pieces of clothing into a backpack handed down from my brother and climbed out the bedroom window. I made my way to the Fremont BART station, crawled under the turnstile, and hopped a train to San Francisco. The Bay Area Rapid Transit system was only a few years old by that point, but our schoolteachers had corralled our class in its silver box-shaped trains to take us on field trips into the city to tour the Kilpatrick Bread Factory or to see *The Nutcracker.* I had paid close attention on those trips—always evaluating ways to escape—so I knew how to navigate the system.

The ride to the Powell Street station in downtown San Francisco took nearly an hour. When I ascended the escalator onto Market Street, the city was teeming with holiday festivities. Outside a drugstore, a Salvation Army volunteer in a red apron stood ringing a bell next to the red pot. A block farther, a man roasted chestnuts over an open wok; the sample he gave me was a gross mush that I promptly spit out. I walked the streets breathing in the cold, damp air, feeling the pulse of undeniable energy. San Francisco struck me as the Holy Land.

Opportunity and possibility hung in the air as tangibly as the steel cables that kept the buses attached to their electric lines. I could find my way out of the chaos and terror my stepfather inflicted. I could escape all of the outward manifestations of my inner shame. I couldn't lose.

All I needed now was a job.

I walked into Burger King on Powell Street and asked the manager for an application. I will never forget the look on this Chinese woman's face. Without a word, she turned around and packed a paper bag with a burger and french fries. She gently placed her hand on my shoulder and guided me outside.

Petite as she was, she bent down to look me in the eyes. "This is a dangerous city," she said. "No matter how bad it is where you came from, it's much worse here. Now, take this and go home."

She handed me the food, her face stern. She didn't call the police or turn me in to Child Protective Services, but the look on her face made it clear that she would if I didn't go home. Her warning only fueled my curiosity. *Horrible danger? Where? Things are happening here, and I want to find out what!*

But I obeyed and found my way onto the next BART train to Fremont, mulling over my soggy Junior Whopper and cold fries. I was sure I was returning to much worse than whatever could befall me roaming the streets of San Francisco.

Back at home, I waited at the threshold while my sister went to find my mother, who I often hoped would protect me from my stepfather, though she rarely did.

When my mother arrived at the front door, she put her hands on her hips. "Really, David? You want to run away and go live on your own? You're seven years old. When will you learn to behave?"

She knew as well as I did what came next—I crossed back over into my role as bad David, and Jim removed his belt once again.

When I was in the third grade, we moved to a larger house in the same area of town, a typical California ranch-style house with four bedrooms and a two-car garage. Jim's job as a cartographer didn't make him a killing, but between his and my mother's salaries, we were by no means poor. And yet, we lived in squalor. I can't even begin to explain why, though Jim liked to blame us kids: "If you weren't such slobs, this house wouldn't be such a disaster."

We only ever managed to hide the mess when we were due to have company, stuffing closets and throwing things into the garage. Most of the time, we lived in the midst of filth. Crusty dishes stacked up in the sink night after night. Piles of dirty laundry overflowed the hampers. Papers and wrappers and lint littered the floors. Our two cats, who lived outdoors most of the time, left mounds of feces beneath Jim's unused desk in the front den.

Our poor dog, who was chained to a post outside, slept in his own feces. Sometimes I took him for walks, an escape for us both. On the side of our house, garbage spilled over the tops of round metal cans, enough to fill a dumpster with papers, old food, and household waste. One of my regular chores was shoveling that gag-inducing pile of shit, cramming it into the garbage cans, and forcing the lids down before dragging them to the front of the house for pickup.

In our new house, I had my own bedroom but remained locked up and restricted to my bed. All of our bedrooms lined a main hallway that ended with my parents' master bedroom. Heavy, dark-blue velvet curtains blacked out their bedroom so Jim could sleep during the day—usually until around six o'clock when my mother came home from work. Sometimes he got up a few hours earlier if he was in the mood to create a little extra chaos. Before that moment, none of us dared make a sound.

My brother, sister, and I knew he was awake when we heard the jingle of his belt buckle, still looped around his pants as he put them back on. That clinking, metallic sound was our alarm system, a storm siren, a first indicator that trouble lay ahead.

The monster had awakened.

If I had snuck out of my room, I ripped back to bed while Shari frantically repositioned the tape along the doorframe. She and Donnie then scurried to their controlled positions out of the way or engaged in a productive chore.

After the jingle of his belt buckle came the clomp-clomp of his square-toed cowboy boots down the hallway on the hardwood floor, like a sound out of a Western movie just before a shootout. My childlike fear amplified these sound effects. The clinking and the clip-clop belonged to someone out to get me. He walked all the way down the hallway until he stood outside my door. Though the sound of his boots had stopped, I swore I could hear his breathing and the angry beat of his heart.

Or maybe that was the sound of my own rapidly beating heart—more often than not, this was a preshift bed-check, and if my sheets were wet, he pulled me down to the floor, yanked his belt from its loops, and beat the shit out of me before stripping my mattress and leaving me to return to bed in the cold. After Jim stormed off to work, I searched for a dry T-shirt or pajamas or an extra clean blanket.

Every day, the stakes of this game grew more intense. I perpetually wet the bed, tried to hide it, and ended up getting caught. Jim seemed to relish his attempts at beating me into submission. I was an animal whose spirit needed to be broken. On any given day, I had six and a half minutes to get home from school and go straight to my room—no television, no afternoon snacks—and if I arrived even a second late, the belt came out of its loops and left its mark across swaths of my skin.

Jim grew increasingly creative in his punishments, an artisan of cruelty, especially when no one else was around to witness it. Once, while I was at elementary school, he found a pile of dirty underwear and wet sheets I had hidden behind my bedroom door. What angered him the most was the black mark the wetness had left on the wood floor. When I came home, he was waiting for me. The next thing I remember, he wrapped the wet sheet around my neck, threw one end of it over the railing on the top bunk, and started choking me.

"I'm going to fucking kill you, you filthy slob," he sneered.

His words were cutting; his actions left me feeling defeated, despondent, neither alive nor dead.

On the occasions my siblings were home, I screamed excessively and begged for someone to intervene. Of course, rarely did anyone have the power. Shari sometimes railed at our mother: "Why are you letting Jim do this to him?" If she acted out or screamed, she too would get sent to her room and told that if she didn't shut up, she'd get a taste of the same.

At times when Donnie tried to challenge Jim's brutality, he got beaten up himself. He eventually gave up, escaping into Little League or Boy Scouts or high school friends—anything other than the drama playing out at home. Before long, my abuse became a family pattern to which everyone grew accustomed. I took on the role of the boy who kept recommitting the same crimes and therefore deserved to be punished.

To pass the time locked up in my room, I listened to music on an old stereophonic record player I'd picked up at a yard sale or read books I'd checked out from the school library—*Charlie and the Chocolate Factory* and its sequel *Charlie and the Great Glass Elevator, James and the Giant Peach*, or *Pippi Longstocking*—not once or twice but over and over again so I didn't have to live in my actual world. Through my imagination, I could escape into the trunk of a tree or the pit of a peach and not be trapped in the chaos of my reality.

In sixth grade, I came across a racier book than those by Roald Dahl, one called *Everything You Always Wanted to Know About Sex (But Were Afraid to Ask)* by Dr. David Reuben, a psychiatrist in California. Before discovering that book, what I knew about sex had come by way of Norman, awkward and age-appropriate sex-ed classes at school, and the things bullies on the playground tended to call me, like sissy and fairy and faggot. My own parents never called me a faggot—they were rather liberal about sex anyway, and by the time I was a teenager, I didn't believe in sexuality at all, nor what everyone else said about homosexuality being wrong or that sexuality was a fixed identity each person was born with. I wasn't gay or straight or bisexual. I abhorred labels of any kind. I theorized that people simply fell in love.

But as an eleven-year-old, my opinions and sexual proclivities weren't yet fully formed, and I read Dr. Reuben's book front to back voraciously. One of the most interesting chapters was on male homosexuality. I later came to realize that Dr. Reuben's original 1969 edition turned out to be horribly damaging to gay men. Like many psychiatrists of his era, he viewed homosexuality as a perversion and a personal choice that could be cured by psychotherapy, and he depicted homosexual behavior as depraved, exceedingly promiscuous, and impersonal. As a chronic repeat offender, the idea of being depraved and perverted seemed alluring. I was already on my way to hell—what did I care?

The part I found most captivating was Dr. Reuben's description of prostitution, how pimps tended to control women and take their money in exchange for food, clothing, and a place to live. *What could be better than having someone take care of me? All I had to do was have sex with men. Sign me up!* I went on to read that male hustlers didn't typically have pimps because they couldn't work as hard or bring in as much money. Even so, male hustlers could still support themselves.

That's what I could be when I grow up—it'll get me out of here. This is how I'm going to escape.

When I was six, I had wanted to be a priest. Five years of abuse later, my prospects had fairly well deteriorated. I was already a hustler—my friend Eddie and I had run rackets all over the neighborhood when we were cute and toothless, and since then, I had raised money selling candy bars car to car at gas stations. Despite all of the ways my stepfather sought to break me down, I was a survivor, one way or another.

Going up against either of my parents was a game I could never win. But there were small victories, like sneaking out of my room in the middle of the night and exploring the contents of our garage, which was stacked to the hilt with a broken-down 1930s Ford pickup truck, motorcycle parts, fishing poles, tools, and endless cardboard boxes.

Jim often brought home tools and technology from his job as a map maker, including films of maps and 3-D glasses before 3-D technology was widely available. He'd had a longtime subscription to *National Geographic*, which he stored in boxes in the garage. On the magazine covers were exotic women in colorful clothing and unusual piercings. Distant lands and faraway wonders. Whales soaring out of the ocean, primates with quizzical looks on their faces. Young boys no older than I was—how I envied them and their lives in the bush alongside giraffes, rhinos, and lions. I creased a tiny corner of the pages I wanted to revisit. Jim, a master of detecting anything I'd touched, wouldn't be able to tell.

On nights when I could sneak into the garage for extended periods of time, I pulled out the maps that came in special-edition issues and spread them out on the floor with great care and precision. India, China, Zambia, Namibia, any place with an unusual name, any place but where I was. I sat mesmerized, wondering what treasures awaited. I dreamed of being an adventurer who would see the world, free to just pick up and go. In my mind, I was already there, a nomad with a backpack. The world would be mine.

Most nights, these dark quiet moments were fleeting. The impending fear of being caught always won out. I carefully returned my dream makers to their place in the banker boxes and snuck stealthily back to my room, an animal returning to its cage. But this dream sustained me day after day, until the time came when I finally found a way out.

CHAPTER 4

Every year, my parents threw a New Year's Eve party, which involved a massive, frenetic attempt to clean up and copious amounts of booze. The better part of the guest list—extended family, friends, neighbors—got sloshed on cheap liquor. The kids were allowed a sip of wine at midnight, but we'd inevitably steal booze while no one was looking.

When I was ten, my first experience of being not-quite-drunk at one of these parties was on Boone's Farm Strawberry Hill, a sickly sweet, lipstick pink pseudo wine and a cultural artifact for those of us who came of age in the 1970s and '80s.

In the midst of the gathering, while I happily played with new friends and kids from the neighborhood, Jim made a crack about my wetting the bed or having an accident at school, something like, "If David would grow up a little and stop going to the bathroom in his pants . . ."—leaving me mortified beyond reason. I lost my mind.

"How fucking dare you!" I blew a gasket, but I felt I could safely say whatever I wanted because I was surrounded by people who would protect me from the inevitable blows. I screamed to the entire room details of what he did to me—the beatings, the choking, the endless assaults. When I ran out of breath, I stood in the midst of stunned silence. Jim glowered at me, hands clenched, knuckles white. He'd have slammed a fist into my face if there had been fewer people in the room.

My mother and Pat, one of her close friends, stepped forward and wrapped their arms around my shoulders. Pat and her husband, Rich, were people I trusted, friends of my parents I thought were cool.

"You're going to be okay, but you've had too much to drink," my mother said, as the two women led me toward my bedroom.

"I am *not* drunk!" I insisted, even as I allowed them to shepherd me into the cool darkness of my bedroom and cover me with a comforter. They sat down on the edge of my bed, and Pat began stroking my hair, moving it out of my eyes and tucking it behind my ear. I would have relished her affection if it hadn't made me realize how deeply I longed for such nurturing, which I never received from my own mother. After they walked out, I was left alone in the dark once again.

Perpetually confined and routinely silenced, I fit in nowhere—not at home, not at school, not within my own skin. I found solace among the potheads and cigarette smokers who hung out at the baseball fields behind my middle school. Like the other outcasts and misfits, I couldn't escape my physical confines, so I tried ways to blot out my mind and awareness instead.

On my way to school, I used to walk through Irvington Park where I once encountered a high school kid named Rod—a bully and a jerk and also the first person to sell me drugs. I usually tried to avoid him, but one day he and his girlfriend were moseying in front of me, wisps of sweet-smelling smoke trailing behind them.

When she noticed me hanging around a little closer than even I was comfortable doing, Rod's girlfriend turned around, holding a joint in a matchbook. "Here, you wanna take a hit?"

I pretended to be casual and cool. "Sure, thanks."

Rod just rolled his eyes. His girlfriend gave me the "in" I needed. I took a big hit of that teensy joint and ended up stoned out of my seventh-grade mind. In the park, I ran into Donnie hanging out with the stoners. At first, he ignored me, but soon he came over and asked what I was doing there.

"I just smoked some weed," I said, "and it was awesome!"

He pulled out a joint, lit it, and gave me a puff.

"Now get your ass to class," he said.

That was the first time I felt a connection with my older brother. And in that moment, I felt like one of the cool kids.

The weed hit me hard. Scrambled eggs for brains, mass confusion, my perspective immersed in fog. I laughed at things that weren't that funny; I sat in a catatonic state, thinking of nothing. When the high abated, I found myself feeling lazy and sluggish, but for the length of the marijuana's effects, I'd been freed of myself.

Rod had other goods, a bag of pills he called Christmas trees. Their nickname came from the green and white beads inside a clear and green capsule. What I didn't know at the time was that these were Dexamyl, an antidepressant turned popular street drug because of how well it mimicked speed.

He sold them three for twenty-five cents. They were cheap, but slow acting. I took a few and declared they were duds—they didn't work. Rather than ask Rod for my money back, which would have ended with my pants around my ankles and my head in a trash can, I scraped up another twenty-five cents. Rod gave me a funny look and forked over another handful. I swallowed a few more, and by the time I arrived at school, I was flying! I couldn't sit still. Inside my body, bones rattled, my entire skeleton engaged in a scrimmage. I placed my hand on my head to push down the hair I was sure was standing straight on end. The feeling was incredible—vibrant, alive. I rode the edge of excitement, motivation, and fear all at the same time. I wanted more. I always wanted more.

At lunch, I went to the grocery store for a soda, and there on a rack near the entrance were what I thought were the Christmas trees in a package labeled Dexatrim. I stole a pack, hoping to make my hair stand on end again. I wanted to be feeling anything but what I was feeling, and that intensity proved a wondrous alternative.

I started selling the pills two for a quarter to my friends at school—for two days, I was a pop-up speed dealer for my seventh-grade class. My friend Mike Jones had an older sister who saw my stash: "These are diet pills! I have a whole drawer full of them!" She'd blown my cover.

Mike Jones was my best friend throughout elementary school and junior high. He was the fat kid with unkempt curly hair. I befriended him, as I tended to do with any outcast in my vicinity. Mike's mom also allowed him to smoke—she bought cartons of Raleigh cigarettes from Sam's Club, and Mike sold the cigarettes on the school baseball field or traded three of them for a joint.

I first met Mike through another classmate who took me to a birthday party at the Jones's house. On a table was a wallet with fifteen dollars sticking out. Not thinking twice, I slipped the cash into my pocket. The next day, I bought cigarettes and a bunch of candy and hid the rest of the cash in my locker.

I was sitting in class when the teacher walked up and said, "You need to go to the office right now."

My stepfather stood waiting for me inside the principal's office. Without a word, he walked me outside.

Before Jim had even mentioned my crime, an immediate lie came out of my mouth. "I didn't do it. I don't know what you're talking about."

"I want you to tell me where the money is, right now," he demanded. "If you don't, this beating is going to be so much worse."

After I confessed to my hiding place, he demanded the combination to my locker. He left me to retrieve the cash, which was about three dollars short of what I'd stolen.

Back at home, he pulled down my pants and beat me until my skin blistered. He intended to punish me so profusely that I'd never steal again for as long as I lived. Once he'd exhausted his anger on my backside, he turned me around and shoved me toward my room.

Later, my stepfather told me, "You're going over to the Jones's and apologizing for what you did. Not only that, you're going to make up for the money you lost and earn that three dollars back."

Every penny of that money mattered—their family was dirt poor, and Mike's mother, Barbara, had been saving for months to buy him a new bicycle. Ashamed, I showed up at Barbara's front door to ask for forgiveness and for the opportunity to earn back what I'd spent.

"Of course I forgive you," Barbara responded.

I went over to their home every day to do housework or rake leaves, chipping away at my debt. In the process, Mike and I became best friends, and his family became a refuge from the terror in my own house. Despite that I started out as the bad kid who had stolen from their mom, their family showed me I was lovable.

The Joneses, being good Christians, took me to church on Sundays. I didn't like going, but I needed the escape, and I could smoke cigarettes and the occasional joint with Mike at their house afterward. This family, filled with laughter and friendship, shared their home with me. They included me in their dinners even though they struggled to feed themselves. I was always welcome at the table. I will never forget that kindness.

My mom had gotten pregnant when I was ten, and after my little brother, Jimmy, arrived, I was displaced from my bedroom and relegated to a wooden cot in the front den in the midst of cardboard boxes and piles of cat shit. While the relocation ended my chronic confinement, I had no privacy, which later proved key to my rescue.

As I entered my teen years, my relationship with Jim only grew more volatile. I had become wild, feral, harder to overpower and dominate. I had grown so accustomed to being targeted, scrutinized, and judged that my reaction morphed into a big *fuck you* to the jackass down the hall. As far as I was concerned, he could take his jingling belt buckle and go screw himself.

Rather than whip me with his belt, Jim had taken to throwing me around and humiliating me in front of anyone in the vicinity. At times, he punched me with his fists. One of his signature moves was wrapping his arm around my neck in a chokehold and dragging me through the hallway when no one else was home, my heels struggling to gain traction on the slick hardwood floor. One of the last hard-core beatings I received, Jim humiliated me by making me pull down my pants first. Mom stood to the side, as usual, cosigning Jim's insanity. I turned to accuse her: "You're really going to let him do this to me?" She flinched with each blistering blow but said nothing.

By then, it was common knowledge in our neighborhood that Jim was an abusive asshole. I had run away to so many different houses that they all knew. Jim inflicted increasing levels of violence until someone in the neighborhood started calling the police to do welfare checks. I remember a handful of visits by various members of local law enforcement—sometimes a pair of guys, or a guy and his female partner, and one time a sergeant stood on the front stoop.

"Please bring David to the front door where we can see him," he said.

My parents never let the cops inside the house. They called for me, and I joined them at the front door.

"Are you being harmed?" the officer asked. "Do you want us to remove you from the house?"

My parents looked at me. What was I supposed to say? Despite all of the ongoing pain they inflicted on my mind, heart, and body, I still wanted them to love and accept me. I responded to protect them and win their favor: "No, I did something wrong, and they were punishing me." Though I'd been put on the spot and showered with guilt, children don't care if we live in a tent as long as we're with our parents. We want their love so desperately that we'll do anything to get it. Somewhere deep inside, I felt that I wasn't enough, but I had to at least *try* to be enough, to do whatever it took so one day they'd give me the love I needed.

Eventually, I discovered who had been calling the police. Sharon Powers lived next door and could hear the ongoing abuse. She was a tiny woman whose arms and body had been withered by polio, and though she rode around in an electric wheelchair, she was by no means meek or feeble. Her husband, Phillip, ran a security business called Powers Private Patrol, and Sharon made it her business to patrol our front window to find out why I was screaming.

In our front yard stood an enormous mulberry tree whose aggressive roots had barreled through the brick retaining wall on the street side of the property. Jim decided to take down the crumbling wall and landscape the yard, and as usual he charged me with the task. He issued me a shovel and a wheelbarrow to remove the broken bricks. The labor was strenuous, but at least I could venture outside.

One day, Sharon came out of her house and struck up a conversation. She pretended she wanted to buy a few of the bricks that were still in good condition, and she asked me to bring her a selection across the yard. Even though Jim was asleep, she wanted to ensure we would be alone.

"I want you to know I know what's going on," she said calmly, "and you don't have to live that way. You don't have to stay there."

I stared at her blankly, pretending for a moment not to know what she meant.

She switched gears to her usual no-nonsense self. "I'm the one who's been calling the police because I can't stand to listen to it."

Apparently, Sharon rolled outside at night and heard Jim beating me through the large, exposed window that faced our front lawn. When she asked questions about what kind of person Jim was, I responded the same way I'd answered the police—I protected him by not admitting what was happening inside our house. Sharon and her husband, son, and daughter were a loving, wonderful family. I didn't want them to know what was going on because I feared I'd no longer be allowed to come over and play. Their house was the closest, easiest place to which I could escape and still make it back before Jim woke up and realized I was gone.

Sharon knew I was lying. "David, I can hear what's happening through the front window. I've had enough. I can't listen to it anymore."

For around nine months of my seventh-grade year, Sharon and I both found reprieve from the beatings after my parents banished me to live with my biological father. Gary and his larger-than-life wife, Ginger, had a son named Bryan, who is three days younger than I am, and two daughters from Ginger's previous marriage, Paula and Sonia. Ginger was a character—she owned an adult bookstore in Stockton. She brought home bags of coins from the video machines that they split up on the table and inserted into cylindrical paper coin wrappers. Stored in the garage were stacks of sex toys and reels of porn films. Their lurid business didn't earn much, but they had enough at the time and were happy to take me in.

Gary was known to be a violent, blackout alcoholic who beat his wife on more than one occasion. Despite his addiction, my experience of him was that of an amazing, caring man who loved his kids whenever he was actually present. A few times while I played with friends outside in the street, he joined us to throw a Frisbee, or he'd ask, "Wanna race?" He wasn't in the best shape, but he could outrun us all.

While I was living with him, he never laid a finger on any of us kids. One day, I got in trouble at school for backtalking my teacher, who called my stepmother. Gary and Ginger had a strong education ethic: "Go to school, get good grades, and don't screw up, or else you won't be anything when you grow up," which contrasted with my mom and Jim's mind-set, which essentially was, "You'll never do well in school. You'll always be a fuck-up, and we expect nothing more."

When I got home from school that day, Ginger glared at me. "When your father gets home, you're in big trouble. Go to your room."

My heart sank. Gary and Ginger had been so cool and amazing to me when I first arrived, and now I was manifesting the exact same treatment I encountered at home—banished to my bedroom and awaiting a beating.

Ginger instructed Gary to spank me and teach me a lesson. He walked in and shut the door behind him.

"I'm going to whip your ass right now, and from now on, you don't talk back to your teacher. You mind your manners and get good grades, you understand?"

He looked dead serious. He pulled his belt from his pants loops. I nodded and awaited the first blow.

"Roll over," he said.

Here it comes, I thought, terrified. *Different father, same beatings.* I felt myself shutting down, retreating inward, steeling myself.

But the first whip was less like leather and more like cream. The lash was so light he could have been simply shooing a fly. After that, Gary slapped the belt against the bed instead.

"Oh, that's not enough for you, huh?" He started kicking me with his foot, and I realized he wanted me to scream so my stepmother would hear me crying and believe he'd really spanked me. I played along, crying out each time the belt bounced off my mattress.

Before walking out of my room, he smiled at me. "You're going to behave at school now, right?"

I nodded, and he closed the bedroom door.

From that day forward, I earned straight As in school.

When I lived with Mom and Jim, I got bullied and beat up at school all the time, every year of my life, probably because

I was vulnerable and weak from living in a toxic environment. The guys in my school called me a faggot, a sissy. They never passed up a chance to throw spitballs at me or turn my jacket inside out or pull my pants down or challenge me to a fight. Such incidents happened all the time—daily, hourly.

While I was with my biological father, despite the drama and poverty, there was no abuse at home or at school. No brokenness. But lots of affection. Ginger would say, "Come here, honey, and cuddle up with me." I'd nestle against her huge, soft belly and melt into her love. Despite how trashy and crazy Gary and Ginger were, they loved each other, and they loved their kids. I basked in the oasis of their affection.

I always felt Gary got a bad rap. He was automatically labeled an alcoholic, an abuser. He never had an opportunity to escape his addiction. I often wonder if anyone ever suggested he get help or attend AA meetings. What I remember is that he received only threats: "You have to quit drinking, or you can't live here or see your kids." I only saw him a handful of times in my life, but he was a fantastic guy when he was around. Looking back, I see a lot of myself in him.

Eventually, Ginger kicked Gary out again. He got drunk, and they fought it out. She threw a pan of hot grease at him, and then he beat her up, right outside my bedroom window. Domestic violence permeated this family like a horrifying illness—a chicken-and-egg situation where it was hard to name the actual instigator. After Gary left, I stayed with Ginger, my stepsisters, and my half brother for several more months. We had to hide from Gary, but Ginger struggled to stay away from him. Sometimes, she would meet him at a bar and bring him home, only to kick him out again.

The adult bookstore eventually closed down. We ended up so poor that we had to evade the landlord. Ginger struggled just to put food on the table. One Super Bowl Sunday, I embraced my inner Eddie McDonald and rallied Bryan to venture into the neighborhood with me to conjure up money for dinner. Bryan and I raked lawns to earn enough money to buy the ingredients for SOS, otherwise known as "shit on a shingle," a mix of starch, grease, and cheap hamburger meat slow-cooked into a thick gravy. We ladled a scoop onto a piece of toast, and dinner was served.

Ginger couldn't afford to keep me, although she tried her best. She was a powerful force, but she had her weaknesses. She never judged me or shamed me or called me names, but I soon ran away again, my sense of brokenness triggered by the instability. I ended up back at home with Mom and Jim for my eighth-grade year, back on the wooden cot, back in the midst of squalor, chaos, and torment.

The next escape from my family was ultimately made possible by the loss of someone extremely precious to me.

My closest friend from childhood was a girl named Gayla Roberts. From a young age, she wore thick Coke-bottle glasses with round black frames. There was a brand of paper towels in those days called Gala II, and kids teased Gayla by saying, "Gala Two, I wipe my butt with you." Her response was to climb down from the monkey bars and punch them in the face. She was strange, awkward, and crazy—and I loved her with all my heart.

Gayla had to grow up fast. Her mother, Martha, was a troubled soul often high on PCP, which we called KJ back then. Gayla was home alone most of the time, so she and I made our own meals and created our own kinds of trouble. By the time we were in seventh grade, we were smoking pot and experimenting sexually with each other. On the nights I snuck out, I often landed at Gayla's house.

Gayla got me a job selling boxes of candy door to door with a group of kids called the Golden Gate Youth Association. Somehow, I convinced my parents I had joined a club for wayward kids that was teaching me to be responsible and stay out of trouble. They bought my story, and I was allowed to go out three to four nights a week. GGYA was no club—that's for sure. We were a gang of outcasts who earned two dollars from every box of candy we sold, and the thirty-something owner, Mike, paid us every night. He had started the operation out of the back of his own van. He secured permits and made up certificates that we gleefully showed at each door while reciting our sales pitch about helping keep kids off the streets and out of crime. Mike agreed to a sixty-forty split, but we had to pool money to buy gas. He picked us up and dropped us off in various suburban neighborhoods that he knew housed middle-income families—the demographic most willing to support local causes. Little did these residents know we were spending all of our money on pot and booze.

On Memorial Day weekend in 1983, the start of the summer before my freshman year, Gayla and two friends were heading to see Stevie Nicks perform at the US Festival near San Bernardino. Gayla and I adored Stevie Nicks. She often put on the record "Leather and Lace" and said, "You're Don Henley, and I'm Stevie Nicks." Sitting on two bar stools, we sang back and forth, though I never quite learned all the words. That weekend, the driver of the convertible carrying Gayla and her friends took a sharp turn off the freeway at high speed to keep from missing the exit. The car flipped on the interstate, and Gayla flew out and was killed.

The moment I found out, I was reclining on the cot in the front den when I noticed commotion outside the window. My sister and a few girls I knew were anxious and upset, so I hurried outside.

Gayla was dead.

At first, I was stunned, and then I broke down—a full-on, screaming meltdown. I couldn't cry loud enough or hard enough to quell the mounting grief.

I walked inside the house where my parents sat watching television in the living room. If they'd heard my wailing, they gave no indication.

"I just found out Gayla's been killed. I have to go—I need to check on her mom."

"You're not going anywhere," replied Jim. "Get back in your room and stay there."

Are you people even human? Are you out of your fucking minds?

We had arrived at a pivotal moment. I saw red, and I called them out on their heartlessness with a fresh measure of courage, a resolve that would finally propel me out of their reach.

"You're such a piece of shit," I said, practically spitting in anger. "Fuck you and everything you stand for."

Before Jim could make it out of his recliner, I turned on my heel and stormed out the front door. I ran straight to Gayla's house. In the midst of all the chaos, Martha grabbed me and held me tight.

"We're going to be okay, baby," she said, again and again, before breaking down into a fit of tears.

Gayla's brother went to the coroner's office to identify her body. The house was bustling with family and friends trying to figure out what to do next. I stayed a couple of nights in Gayla's old bedroom before going back to my parents' house to pick up something to wear to the funeral, which took place within a week after the accident, at Chapel of the Chimes

Memorial Park and Funeral Home in Union City. My parents must have realized what jerks they'd been, because they didn't punish me for taking off. They weren't about to let me leave again, however, so I was in for another fight.

"I'm heading out," I said.

"Oh, no, you're not," said Jim. "You're not leaving this—"

I left before I heard him finish his threat. I stayed with Martha for several days after the funeral. I couldn't go home. I knew I had to find a way out, this time for good.

One afternoon while Jim was still asleep, I snuck into the house to gather a few things into a brown paper bag, and then I called the police and told them I needed to be removed from my home. "If I don't get out of here, he's going to kill me."

By that point, the local police had a record of offenses—the number of times they'd been called to my house to check on me—and this time I had called them myself. Enough was enough. The love I'd been waiting for was simply not available.

After I talked to the police dispatcher, I went outside to wait. Perched atop the crumbling brick retainer wall, I saw the police cruiser approach from down the block before pulling into our driveway.

Out stepped Officer Wright, a young, hip cop with dark hair who had brought me home many times in the middle of the night after I'd run away. He had often lectured me about staying in school and off the streets. I trusted him. In his presence, I breathed a bit more easily.

"Officer Wright, you gotta get me out. I don't feel safe here anymore."

"You realize if you do this there's no turning back?" he asked. "If we remove you from the home, you become a ward of the court."

"Yes, sir. I'm doing it."

"Get in the back of the car."

I slid across the back seat, and he slammed the door shut and climbed behind the wheel. I watched the mulberry tree grow smaller the farther away we drove. Outside, the sky was clear and sunny. Fremont has about as many sunny days a year as Los Angeles, but in my imagination, my entire childhood took place beneath overcast skies, gray and dreary as death. My only memory of sunshine was on that day I finally broke free from the person trying to kill me.

CHAPTER 5

As I sat in the back of Officer Wright's police cruiser, a sense of relief overtook me. I couldn't even muster tears for how wrong the situation was: *I'm willingly choosing foster care over my own parents.* This wasn't supposed to be happening, but I felt a sense of excitement for whatever was next. *Something better has to be coming my way.*

Officer Wright took me to Snedigar Cottage in San Leandro, an unlocked safe house for emergency removals, a place for kids who weren't delinquent but in danger back at home. We drove through a thick forest of eucalyptus trees that opened up to a secluded campus on which were scattered several buildings belonging to the Alameda County Juvenile Justice Center, including juvenile hall and a county courthouse.

Snedigar Cottage was my first stop on the way into the foster care system. When I crossed the threshold, I finally felt safe. I had escaped! I was free, and from now on, Jim could no longer abuse me. He'd been put on notice. Officer Wright escorted me up a ramp into the intake area, where I had to turn over to the clerk keys, money, or whatever else might have been in my pockets. I had very little with me—just a few pieces of clothing in a brown paper bag.

After intake, a good-looking black man greeted me and gave me a quick tour of the facility. Besides the plain white bedrooms, Snedigar Cottage had a living area with couches and chairs and a large game room with a Ping-Pong table. My guide pointed out where we were allowed to smoke and gave directions to the lunch hall. After ticking off the house rules, he said, "Someone will be here to talk to you about placement in a few minutes, so be sure to stay around this general area."

He walked off and turned me loose to a gaggle of kids. Though they were all young teens, they looked aged beyond their years, with worn-out faces and rounded shoulders that carried the weight of the world. Each of them had lived through a variant of the same story—drug-addicted parents, severe physical abuse, mental anguish. A carefree childhood was only an idea we'd seen on TV.

Though I'd never been to Snedigar Cottage, this campus was familiar to me because I'd been to juvenile hall before. I'd been arrested while helping a friend run away from home. While Gayla and I helped this girl carry things out of her house, the girl's mother came home and caught us. She called the cops and accused us of robbing her. When the police arrived, I was walking out with a boom box in my hands. We were all minors at the time, so they arrested us for petty theft.

I stayed at Snedigar Cottage for about three days before officials transferred me to a temporary foster home in Hayward, where I met the angelic and unforgettable Viola Nusom.

Viola and her husband took in about thirteen foster kids at any one time when they needed temporary, emergency placement. The couple, in their early fifties, were a blend of Midwestern values and West Coast liberal hip. Viola canned her own fruit and crafted homemade applesauce. She and her husband also had a round bed in their bedroom, and she liked to joke, "We may be old, but we still get it on." The rest of us just giggled. We knew we were fully welcomed and wholly loved. Her attitude was like, "You're home, you're safe, we got you. Now help me make some applesauce."

The couple also had twin sons in their thirties and a lesbian daughter who smoked a lot of pot and got the foster kids stoned at a nearby park. My new foster brothers and sisters looked like an ad for the United Colors of Benetton—black, white, Asian, gay, straight, pregnant. All of us had been abused, and some came from parents hooked on drugs. Everyone walked into Viola's house with a story, and everyone left at some point for a more permanent placement with hopes of being adopted and taken out of the system altogether.

Viola enforced house rules like being home by a certain time, and once we checked in with her, she wanted to hear about our day and what was going on in our lives. We washed dishes and cleaned our rooms and helped outside in the yard, our chores fair and measured, all of us working together as a cohesive unit. Everyone in that household gave hugs freely. *This is living, and living in love.* On the periphery of our minds were the court hearings and ongoing family drama, but in the meantime, we were safe.

Going into foster care was the best decision I ever made. I felt like I was experiencing real love for the first time in my entire life. I knew my aunts, uncles, and grandparents cared about me, even if Jim and Mom hadn't, but the optics are different when you're living in the midst of ongoing trauma. While living in that situation, I couldn't believe anyone loved me. But once I'd escaped and been set free, I made myself available to love. I might as well have entered Viola's house wearing a sign that said, "I need help. I need love and food and a safe place to live." All my needs were met and then some, and I've never forgotten her for it.

Now that I was receiving proper amounts of love and not fearing for my safety at every turn, my life completely changed. I relaxed among Viola's family and the other kids. I allowed the love to permeate all the fissures in my spirit; I began to solidify, to feel whole. I had a fresh start on every level. I was even going to a new school at the beginning of my freshman year. I remember ironing a bandana that I stitched into a sweatshirt. This was the 1980s, and this homemade shirt was about to be the coolest piece of clothing at my school.

I'd only ever been bullied and beaten up and teased, but for once, I was popular. And perhaps it wasn't the cool handmade clothing, but a shift in my energy that radiated hope and possibility. Not only that, but I could concentrate in class, and I started making straight As. My entire experience—at home and at school—transformed in the light and warmth of this newfound love. I wasn't going to be the same person anymore. I wasn't going to be wrong. I wasn't going to end up black and blue. I wasn't going to be the faggot or the sissy. I had a whole new family. I could be an entirely new person. What a trip!

While I embraced my new life, my old life intruded by way of court hearings and family visitations. Ahead of the hearing that would make me an official ward of the court, my mother had pressured me not to divulge too much about our family life and the reasons I'd asked to be removed.

"You exaggerate everything, David," she said. "You have quite a wild imagination to make up all this stuff you told the police. You're a chronic liar, and everyone knows it."

What mattered most to Mom and Jim was the bill from the state. "If you do this to us," she said, "we'll be on the hook for thousands of dollars for your care."

But at the courthouse, a social worker took me aside. "Tell me what's going on that prevents you from wanting to go back home. You can confide in me, and I assure you I won't tell anyone or allow it to come out in court."

I exhaled deeply. "I do *not* want to go back to that house. I just can't. And you won't send me, unless you want me to return to sleeping on a cot in a room full of cat shit, unless you want me to go back to being beaten to a pulp all the time. If you want me to have that kind of life, then you'll try to reunite me with my family. But if you want me to have a shot at a better life, then send me into the system. I know I can thrive there."

Foster care systems often get a bad rap, and every state has its failings and budget shortfalls and heavy caseloads. But I had nowhere else to go, and I simply didn't want to go anywhere else. My temporary placement with Viola had filled me with such hope. Everything I'd been given—a new school, a family that surrounded me with love, the opportunities to live and be and grow—far outweighed the idea of reuniting with my actual family. I wasn't willing to give up a chance at a better life.

The first rule for wards of the state, however, is to try to work things out with a family in case there is any capacity for healing and restoration. The extent of these efforts on my part included a few awkward phone calls home to check on my siblings. I always ended the call with "I love you, Mom," but she never said, "I love you, too." As far as she was concerned, I'd betrayed her, and now the State of California knew what horrible parents they were. Occasionally, Mom took me to lunch at McDonald's. Our conversations were stilted, quiet, and cold. Sometimes I spent a Saturday afternoon at my parents' house, but I had to return to my foster home by a certain time. Jim stayed away—I'd embarrassed him, and perhaps he knew what he'd done was wrong.

One afternoon, while I helped my mother put clean sheets on the beds (an ironic task), she told me a story from her childhood, how her own mother had been married numerous times, and at one point, she and her brother were put into foster care themselves until her mother remarried and took them out of foster care. I stayed quiet, surprised I'd never heard this story before. She also admitted that Jim had been severely abused as a child—he grew up on a ranch, and his mean-spirited father had inflicted corporal punishment within an inch of young Jim's life.

Eerie parallels, these familial patterns. I could tell my mother hoped to garner some compassion. Her story in no way justified Jim's behavior; on the contrary, I could never feel bad for him that he'd had that life, especially not after he'd inflicted the same on me. How come he hadn't run away like I did? Maybe he thought he deserved it. Maybe he thought I deserved it, too.

I returned to Viola's and remained there for a few weeks before I had to move to a more permanent placement. After my experience with Viola, my new digs were a sketchy letdown. My foster father was a morbidly obese Native American guy who lived with his ninety-year-old mother and ate copious amounts of macaroni and cheese. He was in the process of adopting his two other foster sons, both also Native American. From my perspective, he loved those two boys a little too much. At night, they rubbed his feet while he watched soft-core porn on television.

By then, I'd been exploring my sexuality, and I didn't want this pedophilish man to know I slept with men. Aside from Norman's molestation, I'd had sexual encounters with Gayla, and I'd lost my virginity to Mike Jones's sister, Laura. But while in foster care, I started cruising for guys. One incident occurred on the BART train, where a guy cruised me, and we snuck into the nearest bathroom for a quick tryst.

A more memorable encounter happened while I was a sophomore in high school and living with my foster father. I loved strolling through Berkeley, venturing into bookstores and perusing music at the record store. Whenever I went to Berkeley, I prepared myself to look slick, hip, and cool, like my idol, John Cougar Mellencamp.

One afternoon at the BART station preparing to head back to Hayward, I saw a gangly new-wave trio who reminded me of the Thompson Twins—an older guy, a blonde girl, and a tall, skinny, obviously gay guy with pink feathered hair. The two younger ones had to have been in their twenties—long out of school—while the older guy was probably in his early thirties. The girl started chatting me up, and I engaged with her because I was enamored by how different and cool they were.

"You should come to our house and smoke pot with us," she suggested.

These three new-wave punkers and I took the BART to El Cerrito where we climbed into their station wagon. On the drive, we smoked and jammed and chatted about our love of Tears for Fears and Culture Club. After we'd arrived at their rented house and made our way inside, the older guy gave me a wink. When the other two were busy doing something else, he whispered, "You should come into my room and let me give you a massage."

Fuck yeah. I knew exactly what he wanted, and I was ready.

We went into his room and started going at it. Just then, the other two started pounding on the door and screaming, "You guys get out of there right now!" We froze mid-fuck and held our breath. I could hear my heart pounding in my ears.

"Get out here, right now!" the girl shrieked.

I pulled up my pants and straightened my shirt. The dude finished getting dressed, and we walked out to the living room.

The girl gave the thirty-year-old a laser-hot glare. "We have to talk." To me she said, "You stay right here."

The three of them walked out front, where I could hear them arguing loudly. The front door slammed open again, and the girl blew back into the room, whisking up her bags and other things, and then stopped in front of me.

"Where do you live? We're taking you home right now."

I don't know why all three accompanied me, but there we were, all together in the station wagon—the girl drove, keeping the offender in the front seat. She put me in the far back seat facing the rear window, with the gay guy in the center as a buffer between us. The two of them continued to go off on the older guy for having sex with me. I tried to defuse the tension: "Hey, look, it's really no big deal," but they had no intention of talking about it with me.

By the time we returned to the BART station, I'd missed the last train to Hayward, so now the trio had to drive me all the way home. To make matters worse, I had no idea how to get back to my foster home via the highways. I had only ever traveled by train. I called my foster father and told him I was on my way. I stepped out of the phone booth and handed the receiver to the gay guy, who took down directions.

When I walked into the house, my foster father started asking about my sexuality, perhaps because he'd heard the evidently gay voice on the phone earlier that evening. His curiosity and questioning shut me down. I felt silenced, shameful, dirty. I knew I couldn't stay there anymore.

I had only been there a month, but I told my case manager my placement wasn't working. "I don't feel like I fit in."

My case manager took me back to Snedigar Cottage, where I begged to be taken to Viola's house. In the end, I was only allowed to return to her home for a few days before a more permanent placement opened up.

One day, my case manager came to Viola's house to visit me. "I want to take you somewhere I think you will like. Her name is Rose Holt, and she lives in Union City."

Rose cared for three other foster sons besides me. The four of us slept in bunk beds set up in her converted garage. Though no one could compare to Viola, I loved Rose as well. She took great care of us, and we thrived both in her home and at the nearby high school.

The rolling hills in Rose's backyard connected to Chapel of the Chimes, where Gayla's ashes had been stored in a columbarium. For other people, the nearness to a cemetery might be creepy, but not for me—I wanted to be as close to Gayla as I could get. That nearness to Gayla's remains was exactly why I wanted to live with Rose in the first place; it's where I belonged. I visited Gayla's urn nearly every day after school. Inside the columbarium, I pulled up a couch close to her niche, polished the glass in front of her urn, and wrote letters to her, which I hung on the glass next to her picture—a middle-school yearbook photo.

"Isn't it a trip how God placed me in a foster home on Tamarack Drive right behind you, so that I could come see you every day?" I wrote.

I completed my homework there on the couch and talked to her. I could almost feel her presence, yelling at me about Stevie Nicks songs. "You fucking idiot! You need to learn the words to the songs. I'm going to sing them by myself." I could see her in her Coke-bottle glasses, skirts, and tennis shoes, frozen in time. She was my angel.

Unbeknownst to me, her mother, Martha, had also been coming to visit, and she read one of my letters. One night, around ten o'clock, I heard a horn honking outside of Rose's house. A voice echoed throughout the canyon: "David! Hey, sweetie! It's Martha, Gayla's mom! Where are you, baby?" Martha couldn't tell which house I lived in, so she drove slowly up Tamarack Drive calling my name.

I leaped out of bed and ran outside to find her—she was parked a few houses down.

"MOM!" I yelled. "What's up?"

She jumped out of her car and practically tackled me. I hugged her and held her. We went for a long drive and just cried and laughed.

"Oh, my sweet," she said. "I miss you and I love you. I hope you're doing okay. How have you been?"

I told her about the months I'd spent in foster care and how I would eventually age out of the system and be free to do my own thing. Without a family of my own, I adopted Martha as my surrogate mom. I liked to believe Gayla had played a part in bringing her back to me. We spent time together and took off on little excursions, but eventually Martha disappeared.

After a few months at Rose's house, the case manager once more brought up reunification. I couldn't imagine much had changed at home, but I agreed to a visitation and returned to Mom and Jim's for an evening. We went out to dinner at a nearby pizzeria, and while my parents, Shari, Jimmy, and I sat around a red and white checkered tablecloth staring awkwardly at each other, Jim made a surprising announcement.

"We've decided to move to Missouri," he said. "We'll buy a house and start over somewhere fresh. There are better opportunities where we're going, and hopefully you guys won't get into so much trouble."

The announcement hung over the table for a moment while I pondered my place in this scheme. Were they leaving me for good? Was this their way of saying goodbye?

"Of course, if you want to come, you're welcome. Just let us know," Mom said, looking at me with kindness.

I glanced back and forth between them. Did Jim want me to come? "Are you serious?" I asked.

"Yes, of course. What do you think?" she responded.

How they convinced me to move with them to Missouri, I'll never know, but in the moment, I wondered if I'd had them all wrong. I felt a swell of excitement, a vision of the possibilities. Maybe we could be a happy family after all. My life in foster care had been empowering, but I still couldn't fathom letting my parents down. This might be a chance for us to heal. Maybe they would love me after all. My people-pleasing skills in full effect, I jumped at the chance to show them I was lovable and worthy. My older brother had already moved out, so they asked me to come help them pack and get ready for the movers, who were scheduled to arrive a week later.

I returned to Rose Holt's house to collect my belongings. She hugged me goodbye and wished me luck. Other than that, I never officially checked out of the foster care system or told my case manager I was leaving. Without realizing it, I went AWOL. And rather than sailing into some new horizon, I was walking right back into the mire I'd just escaped.

CHAPTER 6

With Jim's requested transfer approved by the US Geological Survey, my parents packed up and headed to Rolla, Missouri.

It was the fall of 1984, and Madonna's song "Lucky Star" was a hit on the Billboard Hot 100. *Starlight, star bright, make everything all right.* Our caravan across those two thousand miles included my parents, Shari, Jimmy, my stepbrother Trevor, and my mom's dad, Grandpa Willy. Perhaps thanks to Grandpa Willy's presence, my stepfather behaved himself the whole way—no yelling or insults or pulling onto the shoulder of the highway to beat me senseless. I believed for a moment he might even be a new man.

The moving company had arrived ahead of us, and stacks and stacks of boxes filled my bedroom, surrounding the small twin mattress lying on the floor—the first sign that I was still the lowest man on the totem pole. It wasn't long before our fresh start devolved into old patterns. I can't remember the singular moment I decided to run away again—perhaps after Jim attempted to punch me in the face or when he humiliated me in front of the kids on the school bus. It didn't matter. I knew nothing was ever going to change.

I began plotting and planning my way back to California, but I was sixteen with no money and no car of my own. I had no one I could turn to for help. My one hope was the Jones family, but they had few resources and didn't know the extent of what was happening anyway. There was only one person I could think of to ask for help.

Norman, the man who had molested me when I was six.

Several years after he'd shamed me with Bible verses, I sought him out again—during seventh grade, amid the rush of sexual longing that came with puberty and adolescence. During my visits, Norman admitted that he'd been with numerous boys in the neighborhood besides me. As usual, I left with some money in hand. I didn't see him much after that, given my constant confinement and the trauma I was enduring at home. But desperate to flee Missouri, I called 411 from a pay phone at a convenience store near my parents' house and asked for the phone number of the Peterbilt Motors factory in Newark, California. The receptionist transferred me to the parts department.

When Norman answered my call, he said, "Listen, I can't talk to you while I'm at work."

"I'm in trouble, and I need your help," I said. "Is there somewhere I can send you a letter?"

He gave me his address and told me to write him about what was going on. I'm sure he wasn't expecting what I had to say: "Listen, you're going to get me out of this situation, and if you don't, I'll be forced to call the police and take your story to the media. You have to help me."

Several days after I mailed the letter, I called him again.

"You can't keep calling me at work," he whispered.

"Did you get my letter? I need to know what you're going to do about it. This is a serious situation, and I don't want to create any problems."

"I understand. I've applied for an American Airlines credit card. I'll get you a plane ticket to San Francisco, but you can't stay with me."

"Don't worry, I've lined up a place to stay," I said. I had called Mike Jones, and his family had agreed to let me stay with them once I found my way back.

Shari and her boyfriend drove me to the airport in St. Louis, where my ticket was waiting at the American Airlines check-in counter. I boarded the plane for my first-ever flight, hoping I would never have to return to Missouri for as long as I lived.

Norman picked me up from the San Francisco airport and dropped me off at Mike's house, where I stayed for the next few weeks. I tried to find a job but could never secure any steady work. I was sixteen, confused, and filled with shame. I knew I was a burden on Mike's family—they could hardly afford to take care of their own kids, let alone an additional teenager. So, I called Norman again. I was nervous and terrified—I knew he was mad that I'd threatened him and forced his hand, but I felt I had no choice. There was nothing I could have done to protect myself. I had to play this card while I had the upper hand.

When I met him at his apartment, Norman noticed my anxiety and handed me a bottle of hundred-proof cinnamon schnapps. I took a swig and felt a calmness come over me. I'd been stoned on pot, and I'd experimented with LSD while in foster care, but most of the drinking had been just for fun with my friends. We loved to get smashed—we used to steal champagne from the store—but I never identified my drinking as masking my pain. I just wanted to party and say, "Fuck the world!" But after I guzzled that cinnamon schnapps, all of the fear and anxiety I'd been feeling melted away; I was at peace.

"I'm sorry about all this," I said. "I was in a really bad situation, and I didn't know how to get out. I still need your help."

When I told Norman about how badly Jim abused me, he sighed with compassion. "I'll help you get your shit together. We'll find you a safe place."

A friend introduced me to a guy named Roy who needed a roommate. He rented a cheap apartment in the old movie colony Charlie Chaplin used for filming in Niles Canyon—former dressing rooms that had been turned into small apartments with a kitchen and a bathroom—for four hundred dollars a month, which we split between us. Norman loaded his car with spare dishes and towels and dropped me off at the cabin along with two hundred dollars for my first month's rent.

"This is it," he said. "This is all I'm going to do for you. Don't contact me again."

I nodded, and he drove off. I never saw him again.

For the next few months, I tried living as normally as possible for a sixteen-year-old without any adult supervision or assistance. I went to work at Togo's sandwich shop in Fremont, which wasn't enough to pay the bills, so I eventually stopped paying rent. With no family, I hung out with my friends and girlfriend as often as I could.

One afternoon, while my friends and I were crossing a major intersection at Fremont Boulevard, I jaywalked across three lanes of oncoming traffic and came face-to-face with a police officer.

"Young man, that is not okay to do," he said, peering at me with his hands on his hips.

I didn't understand what the big deal was. My friends and I were acting smug and laughing, which seemed to irritate the officer even more.

"May I see some ID?" he asked.

I didn't have my driver's license on me, so he took my name, told me to wait right there, and went back to his patrol car. When he returned, he said, "There's a hold on you. I'm remanding you into state custody."

I couldn't believe it. I'd escaped my parents only to run right back into my legal guardian—the State of California. Soon, I found myself back at Snedigar Cottage, waiting for placement into a new foster home. This time, I wasn't having any of it. Snedigar Cottage was an unlocked facility, so I asked my girlfriend to come pick me up the next morning.

As I walked out, I told the desk guard, "See you later—I'm headed to work." I had moved on from Togo's to a 7-Eleven near my apartment, which paid weekly and demanded long hours. After my shift, I returned to the cabin at the movie colony, but it wasn't long before I got kicked out. The landlord was a fireman who raised greyhounds, and one day on my way to work, I left the gate open, and one of the dogs escaped and was killed by a car. I'd long since stopped paying the rent anyway—that guy couldn't wait to get me out of there.

I needed someone to put me up so I wouldn't end up back in foster care. All I had to do was lie low for one more year and I'd age out of the system entirely. Shortly after I'd returned from Missouri, an old school friend introduced me to his girlfriend, Cheryl Mikel. She was short with brown hair frosted in streaks of white blond—kids at school bullied her and said she looked like a skunk. Cheryl was quiet and intelligent and unassuming. We became fast friends, hanging out a lot, smoking pot and swapping stories. She was an only child whose doting parents, Mike and Lana, agreed to take me in. My case manager, a short Jewish guy, made the requisite home visit to evaluate the Mikel family, but I was so close to aging out by then that the meeting was just a formality.

"I'm going to recommend that you be given custody of David," the case manager told the Mikels, "but by the time that process happens, he'll be too old for foster care, so they'll award him temporary emancipation." He turned to me. "Just don't get in any trouble in the next three or four months, and you'll be fine."

That was it. I never heard from him again.

My life at Cheryl's house afforded me a period of normalcy and belonging I hadn't known before and wouldn't know for many years afterward. I lived in a loft above the Mikels' garage, and though I was technically a renter, Mike and Lana treated me like their own son. We grew very close. I called Lana "Mom," and Cheryl was my sister. I enrolled in a continuation high school and went to class like a normal kid. After a lifetime of being bullied, for once I was finally one of the cool kids, something neither Cheryl nor I had ever experienced. People used to tease us or egg our houses, but no one dared do that anymore.

While living with the Mikels, I often had a girlfriend, including my first true love, Veronica, a skinny blonde who smoked cigarettes and lived with her brother and their single mom. She was everything to me—the sun and the moon, and it was my dream to marry her, have kids, and live somewhere, anywhere, as long as we were together.

I was very happy, lounging around and living a fortunate life. Mike Mikel was a peaceful flower child, a guru-type guy with metaphysical views on the nature of reality. He took us on adventures. Once, we climbed onto the roof where he showed us how to make hot-air balloons using plastic produce bags from the grocery store, straws, and candles. We watched the bags travel high into the sky before the candles burned out.

I could do just about anything I wanted, as long as I stayed out of trouble. I became a wannabe hippie. My friends and I went to outdoor rock concerts and to the beach where we tripped on acid. We weren't intentionally seeking enlightenment, and yet our common bond was one of nonviolence. We cared about each other. We considered each other brothers and sisters. On the beach near Pigeon Point Lighthouse in Pescadero, we circled around a bonfire and tripped on acid or shrooms and smoked pot and bonded by sharing our ideas about the world. Gazing at each other through the flickering flames and flying sparks, we had intense conversations and sometimes bad trips and kept each other company while we tried to figure out the meaning of our favorite Pink Floyd songs.

Tripping on LSD gave us a sense of knowing, a conscious awareness, an understanding of the intense beauty and interconnectedness of the universe. Night fell, and we burned more driftwood as the waves crashed onto the beach. We built the bonfire higher and higher to match our states of mind. Each one of us, alive and present and together. I looked around the fire, knowing everyone around me was experiencing the same thing. *He gets it. She gets it. We're here. We've landed. We're out in whatever.* Nothing needed to be said. Nothing needed to be done. No one even needed to acknowledge what was happening because it was happening to all of us at the same time.

Once the trip faded, we spent the rest of the evening trying to articulate what had happened, but there were no words for the amazing images and sensations we'd experienced. Sometimes those experiences were negative and dark—I'd have a bad trip if I took acid while feeling fear or despair or loneliness or turmoil. But the trips that opened our minds while we remained trapped in a closed universe kept us returning to that circle, seeking more awareness.

After being an outcast for so long, I'd been redeemed by this group of stoner friends, and I loved being the life of the party. Cheryl's parents were very liberal and allowed us to have parties at the house. We had one backyard kegger after another, constantly stoned on pot. The regular flow of alcohol and drugs fueled my addiction, and after a while, Veronica broke up with me. I was devastated. Soon after, my relationship with the Mikels deteriorated. One day, I broke a cardinal rule by driving their car without permission (or insurance) while they were out of town. I drove Cheryl and our friends to the beach, putting everyone at risk. Cheryl's parents were pretty fed up with me by then, and my raging outburst about the situation sealed the deal—I was out.

I rented a room three blocks up the street from a friend named Carrie whose mom, Bev, we lovingly called Ma. This family of four tough-as-nails women refused to put up with any shenanigans—from me or anyone else. Ma agreed to let me stay for a hundred dollars a month until I got my life in order. I couldn't find a job, however, so I started secretly selling drugs to help pay the rent.

Life had gotten better, and now it was about to get worse.

Soon, I found myself strung out on cocaine and four hundred dollars in debt to a drug dealer. His wife, Kelly, was a friend of mine, a skinny twenty-something party girl with a baby at home. She hooked me up with her biker husband, a big-time coke dealer, and he advanced me a supply to sell. But I ended up snorting it or giving it away to my friends because no one ever had any money.

One day, Kelly pulled into the driveway in front of Ma's house. "Hey, David!" she called out. "Come here, I want to talk to you." When I emerged from the house, she narrowed her eyes. "You can't fuck with my husband, you know. You have to pay that money back. I don't care what you have to do to get it."

"I'll get the money, don't worry—just give me some time," I responded.

Shortly afterward, while housesitting for a friend, I broke into his parents' bedroom and stole a collection of gold coins, which I took straight to Kelly's husband—thousands of dollars' worth of gold for a minuscule debt. My friend later confronted me, but I denied it. These people had trusted me to take care of their house while they were out of town, and I'd completely screwed them over. Though I never admitted to stealing, I was so humiliated and ashamed of myself that I could no longer face my friends—this large group of people who had considered me their brother.

Ma knew I'd stolen those coins. She hated drama, and this was serious drama. "It doesn't matter whether you did it or not," she said. "You can't live here anymore. You owe me a hundred and twenty-five dollars in back rent anyway, so you need to move out as soon as possible."

I grabbed a small bag of clothes and called a friend to drive me to the BART station. I hopped on a train to San Francisco with nowhere to go. My heart dropped to my gut when I saw Chris, a close friend who knew the family I'd stolen from. I averted my eyes, but it was too late. The moment he saw me trying to sink into that blue cushioned seat, he headed straight toward me.

"David! I don't know what's gotten into you, but you need to come home and face the music," Chris said.

The train was nearing the Bay Fair stop in San Leandro, so I stood up and jostled past him. "Whatever. I'm not talking to you."

Just before I exited the sliding doors, Chris called out, "We all know you did it, David! I wish you the best of luck with the rest of your life!"

The Bayfair Center, which was called the Bay Fair Mall at the time, sprawled across the area, with department stores, boutiques, and a movie theater. I walked aimlessly through the parking lot, not knowing what to do next, when I spotted a red Mustang II.

A set of car keys dangled from the trunk.

Without any hesitation, I pulled the keys from the lock and climbed inside. Some stranger's mistake was now my ticket out of East Bay. Once again, I'd have a chance to start over somewhere else. Hope collided with terror at the thought that I might get arrested or shot. But I turned the ignition anyway and headed for I-580 to I-5 toward Los Angeles, shaking throughout the entire eight-hour drive. I figured once I got to Los Angeles, I could work the streets and hustle for money. I'd seen plenty of porn—perhaps I could find work as a porn actor. I'd read about prostitution as a kid in the book *Everything You Ever Wanted to Know About Sex*, and I'd hustled with Norman and other older guys during my time in foster care. How hard could it be?

But before I could set foot on the streets, flashing lights atop a highway patrol car flooded my rearview mirror. I was busted.

Grand theft auto.

This time, riding in the back of a patrol car, I wasn't headed for anywhere near as cozy as Snedigar Cottage.

CHAPTER 7

After a few days in the run-down, rat-infested Hall of Justice county jail in Los Angeles, I was released on my own recognizance. As part of my release agreement, I had to promise to appear in court on a certain date, a commitment I promptly dismissed or forgot. I made my way back to San Francisco on a Greyhound bus, which dropped me off at the corner of Market Street and Golden Gate Avenue near the Civic Center. I was eighteen years old, no family, no friends, homeless, penniless, drug-addicted, and facing felony theft charges. I couldn't imagine life getting much worse.

I had been to San Francisco many times—it was well lit and generally safe, even in gritty areas like the Civic Center or the Tenderloin, a district that supposedly got its nickname because cops earned more working the seedy streets and could thus afford a better slab of meat. I wandered the streets for hours with nowhere to go until I remembered that one of my friends from Fremont lived in the city. Teresa was half Filipino and half Irish with long, dark hair. She was also a blackout alcoholic and crack addict who often prostituted herself to get drugs. She ended up being my lifeline during those first few months in the city.

I called some friends from a pay phone to find out where she lived. Teresa and her mother had a flat on Folsom Street, but I didn't realize Folsom ran all the way to Bernal Heights, three miles south of the Civic Center. For the next two nights, I walked down Folsom Street in the freezing, damp April cold, sleeping in random places like one of thousands of vagrants in the city. When you're homeless, it's impossible to get any deep or extended sleep, no matter where you try to rest. Exhaustion clouded my brain. By the time I found her, I was willing to do anything for a bed and a meal.

That's when Teresa told me about hotline hotels: "You know, there's a system in San Francisco. General Assistance will give you a hotel room for seven days. You just have to sweep the streets or prove you've been looking for a job to maintain the free housing."

The moment I heard the word "system," I was like, "Oh, really?"

Teresa accompanied me to the GA office on Mission Street, where I secured a ticket for a room at the Delta Hotel on Sixth Street just south of Market. I'd moved up from sleeping on the streets to a room on Skid Row. This place was disgusting—peeling walls, a crumbling old mattress, dried piss in the sink, rats and cockroaches vying for space among all the drug addicts. But I had a bed and a shower in the hallway. *I'm going to be different. I'll get out of here and make something of myself.*

After settling into the Delta Hotel, I learned where to find free food—places like Saint Anthony's dining room on Golden Gate Avenue in the Civic Center or Glide Memorial Church on Ellis Street in the Tenderloin. Both Glide and Saint Anthony's served lunch from around 11:30 a.m. to 1:30 p.m. I joined a hundred or more men and women lined up around the corner where we waited for a volunteer to come by with a yellow ticket. We stayed mostly silent, a cloud of collective need and shame shrouding us all. Once inside the dining room, I ate as fast as I could because the room was a street stew of crackheads, alcoholics, prostitutes, and people with severe mental health issues.

If I finished my meal quickly enough, I could run over to another place called Martin de Porres House of Hospitality to grab a cup of hot vegetable soup. I rarely went to Martin de Porres, however, because it seemed to me the scariest, most derelict people congregated there. Whether that was true didn't matter. I was in survival mode—there was no making sense of any of my choices. I did what my gut guided me to do. On the streets, I had to get cozy with my intuition real quick. I learned who I could trust and who I couldn't. It was a feeling, not because I really knew anyone—I just knew.

In the various food lines, I inevitably ran into people I had met on the streets, or I would meet someone in line, and in no time, we were making plans to meet up later that afternoon, because what else is there to do when you're homeless? Someone would say, "I know somebody who has a shower we can use." Or, "I know somebody who has some pot." "I know somebody who's getting their food stamps today, so we're going over to his hotel room to get high." That was the culture I found myself in.

Despite a lack of structure, I settled into a particular rhythm of being homeless. Day after day, I wandered a well-worn track around and beyond the Tenderloin, from Polk Street down to Market Street over to Powell Street, up Powell to Sacramento and back across to Polk again. I passed the public library, the park at Union Square, and street vendors displaying stolen goods on blankets draped across the sidewalk. There were liquor stores on every corner, little mom-and-pop shops, and a junk store run by a guy named Art who looked like Jerry Garcia with his frizzy white hair and beard. Art smoked a curved pipe and sold used telephones, coffee pots, extension cords, and other stuff on the cheap. If I came up with anything to sell him, I might earn enough money for a burrito. Sometimes I went early to help him set up the store for a little extra cash.

Walking that track, I was always looking for something to do. I hoped to find someone who would buy me lunch or want to hang out and drink or get high. In those days, I consumed an endless flow of beer, strong and cheap wines like Cisco or Mad Dog 20/20, and as many rum and Cokes as I could get my hands on. Eventually, I would run into people I knew who had alcohol, pot, speed, or some kind of grift that could help me. San Francisco is a very small town when you live in a particular community of people like alcoholics, drug addicts, prostitutes, and the homeless. We all congregated in the same areas because we all needed each other to survive, to get by, to buy drugs, whatever the hustle was.

In those days, there were also adult movie theaters, sex shows, strip bars, and porn stores on almost every corner of the Tenderloin—open doorways with sex toys on display, nothing hidden, nothing to be ashamed of. I found the debauchery in this underbelly of the city lively and exciting. I learned quickly how to navigate the city in search of drugs, alcohol, and sex, because nothing was shut down or hidden away or closed off. It all felt very alive.

Back then, especially before the dawn of the internet, street hustlers—usually drug addicts needing money—walked up and down Polk Street, a road one block east of Van Ness that runs northward from Market Street straight up to Ghirardelli Square. In the 1970s and '80s, before the Castro became the world's gay mecca, the LGBTQ community congregated in the Polk Gulch district at one of nearly a thousand different gay bars. I passed famous places like the Giraffe, Kimo's, the QT, and the Polk Gulch Saloon. The seedy stretch of Lower Polk teemed with drug dealers and hustlers, both gay guys and straight, drug-addicted, gay-for-play guys who spent most of their time playing pool at a bar called Reflections.

The way cruising works is you leer at other men you think are interested, and they signal back. Then, you go into an adult bookstore or get into their car. If you're lucky, you're taken to a bathhouse where you can clean up and have a bed on which to do the dirty deed. At the end of the tryst, you hint at needing money. Prostitution and solicitation are misdemeanors in California, so the way to avoid doing anything illegal is simply not to request or offer money for a sex act outright. If you say, "I'll give you a blow job for fifty bucks," you usually end up with a ticket for solicitation—or worse, in jail. Instead, you say something more general, like, "I'm behind on rent for my room."

My first attempt to turn a trick on the streets of San Francisco was an absolute disaster. Still too shy to walk Polk Street beyond a block or two, I cruised Market Street instead, roaming back and forth outside the adult bookstores. One cold and foggy afternoon, I was sitting on one of the square cement structures that lined Market Street near the United Nations Plaza when I met my first trick—a heavy-set guy with a beard and dark, slimy hair. Not only was he physically repulsive, but he just oozed slithery energy. But I was desperate—I was cold, hungry, and had no real place to sleep.

"You wanna go into the bookstore and play?" he asked. "Maybe I'll buy you lunch afterward."

I picked up his signal that he intended to pay, so I accompanied him into a filthy adult bookstore near the corner of Sixth Street and Mission. He took me to a porn video booth in the back and pulled open the curtain. The fat guy filled up the small space, leaving me hanging halfway out. He pulled down his pants and stuck his ass out. "Now, fuck me."

I was like, *What?* I was super young and stupid. I wondered when I'd get the money, but he just stood there, bent over, waiting. I was mortified someone might see what I was doing, but I pulled out my penis and began to fuck him.

He interrupted me and handed me a condom. "Put this on," he said. Properly sheathed, I proceeded to fuck him again for three or four minutes. He finished quickly and then pulled up his pants and walked out.

I followed him outside and stared him down.

"Oh yeah," he said, pretending he'd forgotten his promise. He reached into his pocket and handed me five bucks. "Here ya go." He walked away, leaving me standing there.

A five-dollar bill in hand, I felt sick to my stomach. Humiliated, a loser, and yet at the same time, somewhat proud that I had actually gone through with a trick. As demoralizing as it sounds, part of me simply said, *Now you know you can do this.*

That didn't mean I was any good at it—I was probably the worst street hustler on the planet. Some guys were used to the risk and felt they had nothing to lose. But I was overwhelmed by fear. For starters, I felt incredibly unattractive—a scrawny, emaciated kid strung out on drugs, competing with muscular Adonises strutting along Polk Street. And I was terrible at cruising. Despite my best efforts, I couldn't get a car to stop if my life depended on it. Every single attempt was a challenge for me.

Rarely would I find someone who wanted to pay for sex—I could count on one hand how many times I successfully garnered a fair amount of money from a trick. Oftentimes, I just walked around all night hoping to find someone to put me up for a bit. From time to time, I would meet an older man willing to take me under his wing and support me for a while. I would soak up whatever he was willing to give until I could go out and get wasted again.

That's how I met Jack, a vintage car enthusiast about twenty years older. One evening, he walked up to me while I was meandering the usual track. "You're really handsome. I'd like to get to know you," he said.

He was simply trying to get me in bed without having to pay for it. I encountered Jack about once a month because he always knew where to find me when he was horned up. He was easy to deal with because he had a micro penis, and he came in about two seconds. Each time, the whole game was about what I could get out of him in return. Jack wanted a boyfriend, so I acted the part in exchange for a warm bed and some food from time to time, and if I came down with a serious problem, I could turn to him in my desperation. Jack was the first in a string of sugar daddies I sought out to take care of me over the years because I was too much of a mess to take care of myself.

Every seven days, I had to return to the General Assistance office to get another ticket for the Delta Hotel, but I only qualified for an extension if I was giving back somehow, like picking up trash or sweeping the streets, or if I could demonstrate I was looking for work. Given that I was a terrible street prostitute, I decided to try finding work through a temporary agency. Jack took me to Goodwill and bought me a collared shirt and tie, slacks, leather shoes, and a funky case that once held some kind of musical instrument to use as a briefcase.

I hit the streets again, but this time, I went door to door signing up at firms like Kelly Services and Manpower, whose staff then sent me on odd jobs like cleaning out basements or assembling binders. One time, I handed out free bottles of

Yoo-hoo chocolate drink to passersby on a downtown street corner. At the *Wall Street Journal*, I filed papers for a reporter who had covered the Baby Fae baboon-heart transplant at Loma Linda two years earlier. I was willing to do whatever the agencies wanted me to do. Though I had to wash my one outfit in the sink every night, I was wearing a tie and working real jobs. I received a paycheck every Friday, which I immediately cashed so I could get wasted or high out of my mind. I often called in sick, but another miserable position always awaited me when I needed to go back to work.

I could never keep it together for long; I just partied until I was homeless again, kicked out of the Delta Hotel for not having a job. With nowhere to go, I ended up back on the street. Once, I camped out on the side of City Hall, where there were vents that blew warm air into the street, and I sat on those all night until morning came.

When I was a kid, in rare moments when Jim realized he had gone too far or done too much damage, he would step back and adjust his take—a punishment would instead morph into a lecture on the tragedy of my wasted life: "It's too bad you're going to end up on the street when you grow up," he said, "because you have so much potential."

I was living out his prediction. At eighteen, I was homeless, a blackout drunk, and selling myself for a meal or small wads of cash. I had fulfilled Jim's vision for my life, and any potential I may have possessed now poured down the street vents I slept on to stay warm.

CHAPTER 8

Somewhere along my daily track around the Tenderloin, I came across a flyer stapled to a utility pole: "Are you homeless? Need a leg up? Make cash daily. Free room and board. Come to the United States Mission." Next thing I knew, I was standing at a pay phone, calling the number from the flyer and asking for an address.

A nonprofit founded in Los Angeles in 1962, the United States Mission had a San Francisco facility at 45 Golden Gate Avenue near Jones Street on top of an adult video theater. A big black guy named Nathaniel greeted me at the door and showed me inside. A flophouse of sorts, the facility had large dorm rooms, a shared shower area, and a kitchen, as well as a street-facing thrift store that sold used clothes and other goods.

The Mission housed only men, about thirty at a time. All sorts of gay derelicts lounged in bunk beds, checking me up and down as I settled in. Despite being totally strung out, I was still pretty cute. Everyone leered at me, like, "Oh, honey, I'm gonna get some of that." I didn't care. I was just grateful to be off the street. I finally had a place to sleep and some semblance of a home life.

Every morning after we'd showered, changed, and eaten breakfast, we loaded onto a giant white school bus that took us to Redwood City in South Bay or Orinda in East Bay. As part of our stay, our ragtag group of drug addicts, hustlers, and ex-cons were required to spend four hours every day going door to door, soliciting donations for the United States Mission, a practice the organization still employs today to instill in their "emissaries" a good work ethic. These donations paid for our room and board and filled a slush fund for extra food or cigarettes.

Some of these guys were highly skilled at solicitation. I heard their spiels again and again: "I'm from the United States Mission—we're a homeless shelter in San Francisco that helps men rebuild their lives." When someone took the bait, the line that closed the deal was, "Checks are fine, but we prefer cash."

I wasn't much good at raising money, but occasionally I started a good conversation with someone, and the bullshit artist came out: "Yes ma'am, men's lives are changed all the time. And yes, I have accepted Jesus Christ as my Lord and Savior. Let me tell you more about the Mission because we are faith-based—" Whatever it took to survive.

On a good day, I might receive a check for fifty or a hundred bucks. Checks had to be deposited in the Mission's bank account, but the other guys were stashing most of the cash they received. At first, I didn't realize they were doing this, and I turned in everything I managed to raise. When I learned the extent of the grift, I joined right in.

As it turned out, I was just as bad at hustling for donations as I was at hustling for sex. I hated asking for money, and my Catholic guilt kept me too honest for my own good. The house manager, another guy named David, told me, "We won't throw you out, but you suck at this." I was young and handsome, so he took pity on me and gave me a job as an assistant cook in the facility kitchen. The head cook was a big fat guy who fawned all over me day in and day out like I was his prison bitch.

While I was living at the Mission, I met Jeffrey Stevenson, a skinny blond guy whose blue eyes peered out of round, black-rimmed eyeglasses. Jeff was fiercely intelligent—when he was four years old, his imaginary friends were Albert Einstein and Nikola Tesla. He was also a paranoid schizophrenic. In his delusion, Jeff believed he was running from the FBI or the Secret Service because they wanted his engineering plans for a fuel-free car, a technology the government wanted to suppress. He told me elaborate stories about hiding from the police while conspiring with other mad geniuses on a top-secret project.

Though I didn't believe a word of his fantastical story, I let him tell it. A lot of people in San Francisco were like that—they lived within a story they told themselves. I just rolled with it because I was so isolated and alone. I needed friendships, and I needed people to like me, and these kinds of guys were harmless. If someone told me they planned to build a spaceship to fly to Mars, I would respond, "Cool! That's awesome. How can I help?"

But I also cared about Jeff and wanted the best for him—he had quickly become one of my best friends. Despite his delusions, he had an advanced metaphysical belief system that I found inspiring. While living in New York City, he had been part of a Buddhist sect that chanted the Lotus Sutra. Though I found the Namu Myōhō Renge Kyō indecipherable, I tried chanting it alongside him during lazy afternoons at Golden Gate Park, hoping for an awakening.

I desperately needed clarity, but at the same time, I was completely strung out and often blacked out. I couldn't control my thinking or my choices—at every opportunity, I smoked crack cocaine, speed, or heroin. I ingested whatever would get me loaded so I wouldn't have to live in my own skin. Unlike my first experience with LSD when I was living at Rose Holt's house—encountering Christ Consciousness and a sense of all-encompassing love and forgiveness—I was no longer in search of that feeling of wholeness. I just wanted to feel okay, and staying loaded meant that I would be okay. I glimpsed spiritual notions of oneness in between long phases of incoherence brought on by alcohol and drugs. I knew these deep truths were out there somewhere, but I couldn't grasp them consciously or in a way that exhumed my spirit from beneath the drug-induced stupor.

One day, I went to a nearby bookstore and discovered a book called *You Can Heal Your Life* by Louise Hay, a Science of Mind teacher and metaphysical healer who helped found the self-help movement. First published in 1984, her seminal book went on to sell fifty million copies around the world. When I returned to the Mission, Jeff took one look at the cover and said, "That is an amazing book. I suggest you read every word of it and practice everything she says. It will change your life forever."

Jeff may have been a delusional schizophrenic, but he had his shit together way better than I did. I was such a disaster, a completely unstable crack addict and blackout alcoholic.

"You create your own reality," he explained. "You manifest your life and the world you experience around you."

I felt reassured that I had some measure of control over my crazy existence. My time at the Mission was during the height of the AIDS epidemic, the most frightening era of my life. Fear seized the city. I just knew I was going to touch the wrong doorknob and get AIDS. I was living on the streets with no clue about my health status, and sometimes I thought I had it. My belief was that I was going to be struck down by this deadly, mysterious disease. Everyone I knew felt that way—the crisis made us crazy. Gripped by that kind of terror, I constantly looked outside of myself for solutions.

In those days, Louise Hay became known for her Wednesday night support groups in Los Angeles, nicknamed Hayrides, attended by more than eight hundred people seeking solace during the AIDS crisis. She had healed herself of cervical cancer through alternative methods, such as affirmations, visualization, therapy, nutritional cleanses (before juicing was even a thing), and—perhaps most astonishing—had forgiven the man who raped her when she was five. Her account of her healing seemed ridiculous and against all known science, but part of me also figured that if I ended up with AIDS, perhaps I could cure it. As silly as that sounds, her ideas were glimmers of hope, a potential tool. I soaked up her wisdom like an antidote for the future, a cure in waiting should the worst happen.

Hay's premise was that everything wrong with people's lives stemmed from a lack of self-love. In *You Can Heal Your Life*, she explained how you could heal your physical, emotional, and psychological wounds through "mirror work," gazing into your own eyes and speaking words of love, as well as cleansing your heart of resentment through forgiveness. "We need to choose to release the past and forgive everyone, ourselves included," she wrote. She also insisted that we must learn to love ourselves. "Self-approval and self-acceptance in the now are the main keys to positive changes in every area of our lives."[2]

Many AIDS activists scorned her and other New Age practitioners as charlatans. Some people interpreted New

2 Louise Hay, *You Can Heal Your Life* (Carlsbad: Hay House, 2004), 7–9.

Age beliefs as blaming people with AIDS or other terminal illnesses for causing their own disease. That angered many people who were hurting and didn't want to listen to any airy-fairy bullshit while their partners lay dying. Unaware and desperate for a way out of my despair, I was drawn in. Besides, I had nothing to lose, and I sensed that this was a tool that could help me.

Every chapter of Hay's book closed with an affirmation, such as, "In the vast infinity of life where I am, all is perfect, whole, and complete. I no longer choose to believe in old limitations and lack. I now choose to begin to see myself as the Universe sees me—perfect, whole, and complete. The truth of my being is that I was created perfect, whole, and complete. I will always be perfect, whole, and complete. I now choose to live my life from this understanding. I'm in the right place at the right time, doing the right thing. All is well in my world."[3]

Sitting on a curb in the pit of the Tenderloin, I read her words and tried to force myself to believe them and to change my thoughts so I could be healed. My mind needed a solution. This was just the beginning of many attempts at trying to repair my broken pieces.

Spiritual teachers often note that affirmations and positive thinking don't have to be viewed as wishful thinking or a metaphysical parlor game, but rather as a way to take advantage of the brain's plasticity and rewire deeply ingrained thought patterns that lead to toxic shame and destructive habits. I needed help and structure, so I wrote down her affirmations—and have rewritten them over the years—a hundred times in different ways. These spiritual seeds were planted

---

3 Hay, 39.

in the midst of my addiction, long before any goodness could break through and bear fruit.

While I absorbed as much of Louise Hay as I could comprehend, I kept asking Jeff, "Can you help me figure out what's wrong with me?" He suggested books from Shambhala Publications and one called *Creative Visualization* by Shakti Gawain, another spiritual teacher who specialized in using the power of the imagination to manifest change.

The idea that my thoughts could create my reality—that I could manifest health, love, and prosperity in my life—was a radical notion at the time. Gawain had a meditation on cassette tape called "Creating Your Inner Sanctuary" in which she guided the listener through visualizing a safe, serene mental retreat, a starting point from where you'd then visualize your ideal future, the life you wanted to create. She suggested places like a meadow, the forest, or a beach, anywhere pleasant and peaceful. For whatever reason, my sacred inner sanctuary was a spherical bubble perched on the north tower of the Golden Gate Bridge, overlooking the San Francisco Bay and the Marin Headlands whose lush, green hills roll along the rocky Pacific Coast. I returned to that image again and again—during my addiction, I retreated to this inner refuge during moments of severe paranoia, and I still use it from time to time.

My attempts at manifesting goodness and prosperity in my life through creative visualization were sabotaged by an opposing inner force—the voice of trauma and brokenness: *You're not good enough. You're never going to make it off the street. Your life is shit—you're a prostitute. You're not worth anything. Just look at what you've done.* The only way I knew to escape that voice and the suffocating experience of being inside my own body was to get strung out on crack or drink myself into oblivion. Before long, I bottomed out completely. I no longer lived at the Mission. I couldn't find a pseudo boyfriend or sugar daddy to take care of me.

One night, strung out with nowhere to go, I roamed the western edge of Mission Dolores Park along the Muni Metro J-Church tracks, a section known for cruising. I had just sat down on a bench near a cluster of trees when someone emerged from the foliage. Henry, the manager of a performing arts venue, was one of the older men I bonded with and often sought out during those years. He was a highly spiritual person with metaphysical views similar to what I'd been reading in the books by Louise Hay and Shakti Gawain. He had filled his apartment with crystals and gongs and bells, and he encouraged me in my spiritual practices.

He lived near Dolores Park, and I often met him there, so it was no surprise to me when I ran into him that night.

"Hey, David, how are you?" he asked, his tone gentle and sweet.

"I'm good." I pretended I was fine. This was my game—I didn't want anyone to know I was homeless, that I had no money, that I needed help. I just wanted to get into their house, get some food, maybe have some sex, and get a shower.

Back at Henry's apartment, I explained how I needed money to get to Missouri. The last thing I wanted was to return to my parents' house, but I saw no other option. I had learned that the social services agency would buy me a bus ticket and give me five dollars a day for food, but I needed more money for the five-day trip.

Henry interrupted my sob story. "We're not going to have sex. I want to talk to you about how you're seeking your father in me, and I'm not your father, and I'm not going to take care of you. I'm not going to do that." He showed me a chapter in a book he'd been reading about personality types. "This is you. It all makes perfect sense."

While I recognized an element of truth to his statements, I knew the sugar daddy was an available archetype I could use to my advantage when I needed someone to take care of me. I also thought I was much smarter than Henry gave me credit for.

After itemizing my codependent behavior patterns, he said, "I'm not going to save you. What you need to do is call your parents, right now, from my phone, and tell them your situation."

Are you fucking kidding me? Throughout my life, my parents were a proverbial well I kept returning to for love and sustenance, only to find it dry and empty. What good would it do this time?

"Here's the phone. Call your mom."

I sat forward on the edge of Henry's couch and dialed the numbers on the keypad. When I heard my mom's voice on the line, I told her how strung out I was and how hopeless I felt.

"Why are you doing that, David?"

"I don't know." Throughout that period of time, I believed the drugs were due to the molestation, my deepest secret.

"What do you need?" she asked.

"You have to be home to answer the phone and tell social services you'll be there to pick me up when the bus drops me off in St. Louis."

"Okay, we'll do it."

"Is Jim okay with it too, then?"

"Of course," she said, a hint of resignation in her voice.

I arrived in Missouri with my stuff in a black plastic garbage bag and my tail between my legs. My parents had moved to a new house I'd never seen before, but under the bed in the room they stuck me in were masses of dried cat shit, just like the front den in Fremont where I'd slept on a cot. I couldn't believe it. Once again, I was right back where I was before. My sojourn in St. James, Missouri, lasted about four weeks before I encountered more of Jim's unbearably abusive behavior. Angry and in tune to him, I knew what was coming, and it wouldn't end well.

I left with my trash bag of belongings and moved in with Shari, who had rented a small farmhouse about a mile from our parents. Not only was she glad to have me, but I think she gleefully expected it. Shari was a strong young woman who had two sons by then, Craig and Jacob, who were so much fun to be with. Jimmy often hung out with us as well. I landed a job at a shoe factory in nearby Steelville, and while I was still too close to my parents for comfort, living with Shari felt sustainable for the time being.

I started calling Jack in hopes that he would bring me home to San Francisco, if only for a visit. I wasn't really into him, but he was an incredibly wealthy man who could afford opportunities I couldn't get on my own. I pretended more and more, hoping he would give me more, but little did I know he was cheap as fuck—he was never going to give me anything. When he suggested I come stay with him for a "trial run" on a relationship, I flew back to see whether I'd "qualify" to be his boyfriend, Jack's ruse for more free sex.

What happened next is comical only in hindsight. Back in San Francisco, I went out one evening to meet up with Jack and a friend of his for a movie. The two of them were standing near a bus stop across a busy intersection. As the light began to change, I raced across the intersection to beat the yellow light. Just as I neared the curb, a car pulled into the crosswalk in front of me. I jumped over it, my hand slamming into the hood.

As it so happened, a couple of police officers were parked near the bus stop and heard me hit the car. "What are you doing! That's totally dangerous—you could have gotten killed."

They asked for my name and identification. A wicked moment of *déjà vu*, a flashback to being accosted at seventeen in Fremont and sent back to Snedigar Cottage. Only this time, rather than discover I was a ward of the court who had gone AWOL, the officers found a bench warrant for failure to appear in court for felony grand theft auto. They arrested me on the spot, and soon I was sitting handcuffed in a sheriff's department bus en route to Los Angeles to face the judge about the stolen Mustang II.

And, naturally, the boyfriend situation dissolved just like that.

CHAPTER 9

Back in Los Angeles, I was processed into protective custody in the Hall of Justice, a horrible facility with leaky pipes and rats that scurried over dirty floors. The only amenity to speak of were windows that allowed us to see outside between long black iron bars. My public defender managed to reduce the charges to misdemeanor joyriding, but what did me in was my failure to appear.

The judge sentenced me to 120 days: "You were a fugitive of the law for over a year. You didn't even try to get in touch with the court."

Being in jail was almost a relief. I had a bed to sleep in and food to eat every day. I wasn't trying to get loaded or tracking down a sugar daddy to put me up for the night. As much as I wished I weren't incarcerated, I always thrived in a controlled environment. I'd had the same experience whenever I was locked up in juvenile hall, assigned to a foster home with established rules, or enrolled in a school with strict structure. I did well when I knew what the rules were. I knew if I followed the rules, I would be okay.

I was released after sixty days. Jack bought me a bus ticket back to San Francisco, but he wouldn't let me stay with him. Once again, with nowhere else to go, I was forced to return to Missouri. This time, I knew better than to live with my parents, and I couldn't see myself making a go at Shari's again, so I stayed with a friend instead. I migrated to St. Louis in search of better work opportunities, where I landed a few jobs, including a stint as a line cook at Southern Air, Chuck Berry's former restaurant. After that, I went to work as a bus boy, and later as a server, at Maggie O'Brien's Irish Pub, where I celebrated my twenty-first birthday.

On October 17, 1989, the Loma Prieta earthquake hit sixty miles south of San Francisco at a 6.9 magnitude, devastating the city. The images on television of leveled, burning Victorian buildings and sections of the Bay Bridge, buckled and crumbling, shocked me. I missed California more than ever. I called to check on Jack, who suggested I come back and live with him after all. In San Francisco a few weeks later, I attempted some semblance of a normal life—as normal as possible given that I was a blackout alcoholic and willing to snort up just about anything to get loaded. As an addict, all of my relationships tended to be rather volatile, and at some point, after one fight or another, Jack kicked me out.

I returned to the Delta Hotel on Sixth Street, and in order to maintain the free housing, I went back to temping for Manpower. This time around, I had to better manage my drinking and using—I just had to. The staffing agency sent me to Charles Schwab at 101 Montgomery Street in the Financial District to be a gofer for the firm's number two man—Hugo Quackenbush, a colorful personality with a deep, dramatic voice. I filed papers and ran errands to various departments within the building, electronic key in hand to get past all kinds of security measures.

For once, I saw an opportunity to finally make something of myself—I considered this bottom-rung temp job a stepping-stone to a career in financial services. No more menial, disposable jobs. No more trying to hustle on Polk Street. No more dependency on sugar daddies. I would defy my parents' dire predictions. At long last, I had a measure of hope for my future. I just had to work hard and bide my time.

Other employees noticed my efforts and gave me tasks to complete, like putting together three-ring binders for a handbook of some sort and then manning a customer service phone line. One day while I was working the switchboard in the operations room, connecting incoming calls to stock transfer agents, I overheard two female managers—one of them the woman who had put me to work on the three-ring binders—talking about an open temp-to-perm position in her department.

I interrupted them. "Oh, I'd love to get in on that."

"You totally can," she said. "You're a great worker, and we really like you. Come back tomorrow, and we'll talk more about it."

Soon, I became a temporary stock transfer agent with the option to go permanent after a certain period of time. My supervisor moved me to 333 Bush Street, the building that housed the stock transfer department. The job entailed data entry of a stock sale from one owner to another, issuing and mailing stock certificates to clients, and keeping track of their accounts.

During those first few months I worked for Charles Schwab, I met a man named Edmund while I was out one night, partying at a local bar. He was from Boston and managed a small hotel called Classic Suites. We went home together that night, and the next morning, I asked him, "Do you think I could move in with you?" Anything to get out of the flea-bag hotline hotel. He said yes, and soon we were not only dating but bunking together in a little apartment near the United Nations Plaza.

At last, I was moving up in the world—I had a real job, an actual boyfriend, and a nice place to live. For the next year,

I mostly kept it together. On weekdays, I wore a suit and tie to my job at Charles Schwab, and on weeknights, I worked hard to manage my alcoholism around Edmund. I had a somewhat normal life for once, and I didn't want to mess any of it up. I still drank lots of alcohol, but I didn't use a lot of drugs. Edmund and I partied with a gaggle of friends on the weekends, taking Ecstasy at dance clubs, but I didn't go crazy or get cracked out.

My goal at Charles Schwab was to get my Series 7 license through their in-house training program because this was the only opportunity that had come my way, and I planned to seize it. I would be a trader and work on the stock exchange. After a year of working as a temporary stock transfer agent, my supervisor announced I was eligible for permanent employment. To qualify, I had to take the Series 7 test and be bonded for $5 million.

The process, however, also included a criminal background check.

I knew what they would find, and I wasn't sure how to handle it. Should I confess the truth about the Mustang II and risk ruining my one feasible opportunity? Maybe I could downplay the whole incident and just move on. Hadn't I worked hard for a whole year? Would it really matter?

The day of the interview, I met my manager and two of her subordinates in a conference room. It didn't take long for her to bring up the joyriding charge they had found on my record: "Can you tell us about this?"

I had no idea what kind of details the background check revealed—all I knew was my past had caught up with me and now threatened the future I'd been counting on all year long. I decided my best bet was to downplay the crime and hope my manager wouldn't press the issue.

"Yes, well, I was actually just a passenger in the car when that happened," I said.

Her face fell. She knew I had outright lied. Who knows what might have happened if I had told the truth? Either way, it was all over.

"I'm sorry, David, but we're going to have to let you go."

That singular lie changed the trajectory of my life forever.

Back at home, I could barely find the words to tell Edmund I'd just lost my dream career opportunity. Not only that, but in the weeks that followed, I couldn't seem to find another job anywhere, especially not in the financial sector. I started drinking heavily and using drugs again, returning to the four-mile track I used to roam when I was homeless. Same scene, same stores, same hustlers in the same places. That's how I ended up running into Jeff Stevenson, though I hadn't seen him since I left the United States Mission. But just like old times, we picked up right where we had left off. We found a cheap sandwich shop and sat down for lunch.

"Oh my God, what are you doing—you look great!" I said.

He did look great. He was cleaned up and healthy—he evidently had some money and had his shit together. I told him how I had no job and no opportunities and no idea what to do.

"I could help you," Jeff said. "I've been sharing an apartment in the Mission, and I've been doing massage—I put ads in the BAR."

The *Bay Area Reporter* is a free weekly newspaper that serves the LGBTQ community in San Francisco. Jeff pulled out the latest edition and flipped to the back, which featured want-ads for jobs and roommates and personals of all kinds, including escort services and erotic massage. I'd seen these ads plenty of times.

"Look," he said, "this is my ad. I've been charging fifty to seventy-five dollars a session."

At the time, fifty dollars was a goldmine to me. Jeff showed me the pager clipped to his belt that he used to receive calls. "You need to do this—you're giving it away for free all the time anyhow. I can show you how to do three different kinds of massage, and you can use my room to see clients. I want to get out of the business anyhow now that I have a boyfriend."

Jeff described his new lover, a spiritual older man named Kajetan. Kaje, as Jeff called him, dealt in luxury real estate and lived in a penthouse apartment overlooking the Palace of Fine Arts in the Presidio. Kaje studied and practiced Buddhism, and Jeff had been a longtime practicing Buddhist himself, so they immediately hit it off and started sharing a spiritual journey.

"I have it made now," said Jeff, "so let me pass this on to you." He handed off his PageNet pager and twelve bucks for my first ad in the BAR, along with keys to his place on Sycamore Alley in the Mission so I had somewhere to meet my clients.

I was thrilled—I had a way out. I ran my first ad for erotic body massage the following week, fifty bucks for an hour-long session. The newspaper came out every Tuesday, so that first Tuesday and every week afterward, my pager beeped off the hook. When I called the number on the tiny screen, someone would ask, "Are you available now?" or "Can you meet in an hour?" or "Will you come to my house today at three?" Armed with that precious pager and a gut instinct that still doesn't fail me to this day, I was off to the races.

Jeff had shown me three simple techniques for deep tissue, Shiatsu, and erotic massage. He demonstrated opening moves to get the heat moving through the body, the muscle areas to target for deep tissue and acupressure, and how to work my way down one side of the body and then the other. This part of the massage lasted maybe thirty minutes, and then I rolled the client onto his back. At this point, the client would grab me or rub me, a signal that it was time to get them off and get them out of there so I could move on to the next appointment.

Many of my massage clients were good-looking guys, sometimes fresh from the gym. Others were older men who wanted to have a massage and get off at the same time. Most of these guys wanted a certain experience without having to go out to bars or appear to pay for sex. Some of them didn't even want anything erotic, which meant I had to work at giving them an actual massage—those were the most difficult. I saw about three to four clients a day, which meant up to two hundred dollars a day, which was a fortune to me at the time. Not only was I able to buy alcohol, but I could buy food and clothes and whatever I needed to survive.

I stayed in touch with Jeff. He often came over or we went out and partied, once I was making a little money. One night when we were hanging out, he said, "You're not doing massage—you're doing escort work and charging massage rates. You have sex with every guy you massage. Why give fifty-dollar massages when you could be turning tricks for a hundred bucks?"

I didn't think I was good enough—I always thought an escort had to look like a porn star. "I could never do that. Those are real professionals. I'm not handsome enough—I don't have that Adonis body."

"Don't be ridiculous," Jeff said. "You'll be great. What's more, you make your own rules, and you can pick your own clients. You don't have to see anyone you don't want to see."

With trepidation, I took his advice and placed an ad in the BAR for adult services starting at a hundred dollars an hour. To hide what I was doing from Edmund, I changed the name in my ads to Jon, and I was on my way.

I often found myself running to the pay phone, answering random pages to go see some mysterious person on the other end of the line. The risk was enormous. Given the AIDS epidemic, those were dangerous days. Clients often called from one of the many run-down and dirty motel rooms around the city, and there was no telling who might be on the other side of the door. I was excited and terrified at the same time. I grew used to the sheer terror of being alive in San Francisco, a hotbed for the lethal disease, a gay man having sex and selling sex, while friends and acquaintances dropped dead left and right. I was convinced I would be infected any day and drop dead myself.

Hope had emerged a couple of years earlier—AZT, an antiretroviral medication, received fast-tracked approval from the FDA in 1987, a poison that managed to sustain people's lives a little while longer. But the drug was difficult to access; there was a two-year waiting list, and treatment cost eight thousand dollars a year. Plenty of people died before they ever got their hands on a bottle.

The gay community lived and moved in a shroud of heavy gloom. The rest of the world blamed us for the disease, calling us immoral sex maniacs who were receiving our just punishment from God. The virus brought us together as a tribe united against rejection and judgment, and yet it also tore us apart—we were self-hating and fearful of one another, inspecting every mole and crevice on another's skin, questioning why they were so skinny, wary of getting close.

One afternoon, my pager went off, and knowing I'd soon have some cash in my pocket, I ran to the pay phone to call the client.

A quiet, husky voice came on the line. "Are you coming over or not?"

Confused by his abrupt demand, I said, "Why are you asking me this? I don't even know who you are."

"You said you were coming over, but you haven't been over here yet. I've been waiting for you all day."

"I haven't gotten any pages or talked to you at all today."

"Well, are you coming over or not?"

"It would help if maybe you told me where you live."

We had this whole argument, and I was so desperate for money to get high that I didn't care that the guy sounded half crazy.

At the time, I had to pay extra to have a picture of myself in the paper, so no one knew what I looked like. A caller interested in hiring me would usually ask for a description. I would say, "I'm five eleven and a hundred and thirty-five pounds. I'm usually a top and rarely a bottom," some spiel already laid out. I never described an actual sexual act but rather said, "I'm open to most scenes." It kept us away from the obvious legal issues. But I had agreed to go to this guy's place without even discussing money or what he was into.

He lived in a condo at the top of Corbett Street in Twin Peaks. The 37 Corbett bus dropped me off at a wooden staircase that climbed forever up a steep hill. I walked up the interminable steps to his building and rang the doorbell. A few seconds later, I could hear coughing and heavy breathing and the shuffling of feet. When the door opened, standing in front of me was a man not yet thirty but already a living skeleton draped in wizened skin. Wisps of hair on his bare scalp flickered in the late afternoon breeze. I knew instantly I was looking at a man dying of AIDS. *Oh my God.*

"Are you okay?" I asked.

This dead man walking spoke weakly through dry, cracked lips. "Yes, of course I'm okay. Are you coming in?"

"I better not." I knew what was happening to him, and it terrified me.

"Please stay," he pleaded. "I need your help with something."

"I think I should go."

"C'mon, please stay." He stood there in hospital pajamas and a thin cotton robe. Tears began streaming down his cheeks, his face clenched in anger.

Despite my terror, I felt incredibly sad for him. His palpable loneliness drew me in, and I agreed to go inside. Half of me was there simply because I needed some money, but the other half kept screaming, *What the fuck are you doing?*

I followed him down the front hallway. His home was dirty and unkempt. Dishes piled up in the kitchen sink, and the air smelled like baby vomit.

"No one comes over anymore," he said. "No one wants to touch me. No one wants to be anywhere near me—not even you. You don't fucking care." He turned to face me, a look in his eyes that dared me to prove him wrong. He was so angry and confused, and his pain was so heavy I could feel it in my bones. "I just want to be touched! I want to be held, just for a moment. Please, fuck me!"

Deep in my being, a part of me surrendered. I couldn't begin to imagine what he was experiencing. My head swirled in disbelief. Part of me panicked, another part of me just ached with heartbreak. I gathered my senses and put my own emotions in check. I didn't want this man to feel untouchable, not even for a second.

"Look, let's just lie down and let things happen naturally," I said. "No rush."

I eased him onto his unmade bed, moving the covers so he'd stay warm. I stretched out beside him and wrapped my arms around his emaciated frame. His lungs crackled with each breath. Despite that I had acquiesced to his wishes, he kept getting up and throwing another fit about how nobody wanted him. I just brought him back to the bed each time, taking him into my arms again.

My thoughts kept wandering off—out of my body and then back into the room again. Though I felt present in the moment, my addiction was calling, constantly interrupting, beckoning me to fill the vast hole of emptiness inside.

Over the next couple of hours, I helped him clean up and brush his teeth, and I changed the sheets on his bed. Since I was an incorrigible alcoholic, I always carried around a small, flat bottle of peppermint schnapps, which I pulled out of my pocket and handed to him. He took one swig and then vomited all over the kitchen floor.

"Someone can't hold his liquor," I said, giggling and trying to ease our embarrassment.

"Obviously." He shrugged, resigned to his reality.

In that moment, he just looked at me with vulnerability and tenderness. I could discern the fear and sadness in his face. I could tell this was the moment he became aware of himself and his own fragility. He walked toward his bed.

I'd been peeking around his apartment to see whether he had any money or something I could steal because I knew the monkey on my back would soon become a gorilla. Not seeing anything of value, I turned the conversation back to bitter reality.

"You know I'm an escort, right?"

He seemed to regain some of his power. He responded sharply, "I'll tell you right now I don't have any money, but I have some drugs."

My eyes lit up. Maybe this had been a good call after all. He pulled out a baggie that was supposed to be crystal meth, but it turned out to be baby powder—someone had been there before me and had taken advantage of him. That solved the mystery of who was supposed to come over all day. All my hopes collapsed. The gorilla was beating his chest—the call of drugs grew louder. I had to get out of there.

We finally lay down again. I held him for a while until he fell asleep. When I started to leave, he woke up. I had to tear myself away.

"I have to go. I have things to do," I said gently.

I was jonesing hard—I had to get high. My body trembled, and my mind raced. *Just one hit, and I will be okay.* He started to ramble and then fell asleep.

When I walked outside, I felt changed. I felt different. The sadness of that experience wrecked me. I roamed the streets, shaking to my core. I finally found a friend with some crack, and once again, I surrendered to the oblivion.

Those mundane hours with this total stranger, someone dying alone from AIDS, informed my entire response to the epidemic. This encounter penetrated the dense cloud of my addiction, my ignorance, and my ability to blot out the truth. Awash in this dying man's loneliness, I discovered a new depth of compassion. I knew I would never let anyone die alone like that. The fear of touching or holding or being close to someone with AIDS simply vanished.

CHAPTER 10

One evening, a man named Mitchell paged me and asked if I would come over and stay the night. Mitchell was a beautiful blond with a great body and a gentle demeanor. He managed a retail store and lived in a nice apartment in the Upper Market with his partner, who was conveniently out of town that evening. When I arrived at Mitchell's place, his coffee table displayed all kinds of paraphernalia for injecting crystal meth. Turns out, he wanted me to help him shoot up.

I'd snorted crank as a kid, a low-grade form of speed we used to call poor-man's meth, which wasn't as addictive. I'd always heard that shooting up crystal meth was selling your soul to the devil. Everyone I ever knew who shot up became a junkie. For years, I'd been entirely against it—until now. Given my situation, I felt like I didn't have much left to lose. In fact, though I'd never shot up meth before, I was more than happy to try.

Plopping down on the couch next to Mitchell, I surveyed his supplies. He had a couple of syringes, a shot glass, and a few cotton balls. Inside a clear plastic quarter-gram baggie with tiny black spades across the bottom were transparent shards that looked like ice. He splashed some water into the shot glass and mixed in crushed crystal until the powder had completely dissolved. He dropped a pinch of cotton into the mix to strain out any impurities or stray lint or hair, and then he tilted the glass until the cotton had absorbed all the liquid. He stuck the hypodermic needle into the tiny ball of cotton and sucked up the liquid into the syringe.

Mitchell had a tourniquet for tying off his arm, but I didn't need it—it was so easy to stick myself. Following his lead, I stuck the needle in a vein, pulled the syringe back just enough to see a bit of blood in the syringe, and then plunged it the rest of the way in.

My first reaction was to start coughing, and my eyes started watering. But the second that crystal meth hit my system, all of my problems were solved. This was it! I had sought out so many other drugs to escape being in my skin, and I'd finally found the holy grail. No longer a blackout alcoholic, no longer a cracked-out cocaine addict, I was whole, complete, and home. I was invincible. In tune, hyperfocused. Intensely aware of every sensation, sound, color, and detail, I felt pure amazement.

Mitchell and I spent the rest of the night randomly shooting each other up and having sex in an alcove that functioned as his bedroom. All inhibitions (what few we had) dropped away. The drug turned Mitchell into a sex-starved bottom—he couldn't get an erection and wanted instead to be fucked nonstop for hours. For me, shooting meth made me rock-hard and a nonstop top. Later, this seemed like a blessing for my sex work, but anyone who found out I could be a fully functional top while high on meth would want to keep me high, which made quitting much more challenging.

Shooting crystal meth sends the drug straight to the brain—a quick and powerful rush. A soul-stealing drug, this new high utterly consumed me. Nothing like the bathtub crank I'd snorted as a kid—this was pure, pure, pure, and I was addicted from the start. Within a week, my meth usage was completely out of control. And I didn't stop using for the next twenty years.

For a while, I managed to hide my illicit life from Edmund. I wore long-sleeve shirts to hide the track marks. I came home late at night and soaked my arms in the bathtub. But I wasn't as good at hiding my addiction as I hoped. All of the friends I'd made through Edmund and while working at Charles Schwab backed away when they found out I was escorting and strung out. Edmund loved me enough to remain in denial until he just couldn't anymore.

One day, I received a page from a number that looked vaguely familiar. When I returned the call from a pay phone, the voice on the line asked, "Is this Jon?" He had a distinct Bostonian accent.

"Who is this?" I asked.

"David, we need to talk."

Oh, shit. I was so busted. Edmund knew my pager number from when I was doing massage, but that number had since been attached to escort ads in the back of the BAR.

"Come over here, right now," he said.

I walked over to Edmund's office from wherever I was. Through a large street-facing window, I saw him standing over piles of newspapers spread across his desk. His hotel was one of the drop points for the BAR. He had three weeks' worth of the adult services ads laid out in front of him.

When I walked in, he glared at me. "You want to tell me about any of this?"

I paused, pondering a response. But before I could open my mouth, I just took off. I couldn't face it. I left, and I left him. One of my friends later convinced me to go back to Edmund, but we ended up in a huge drunken brawl, so I took off again. Jeff had given me his room in the three-bedroom apartment on Sycamore Alley to use for massage, so I went to stay there for a while, sleeping on a futon mattress on the floor. I never saw the other two guys who lived there.

While I was on Sycamore Alley, no one ever paid the phone bill, so I still had to run out to a pay phone every time my pager went off. One night, Jeff paged to tell me Kaje wanted to take us to dinner. I hadn't yet met this elusive wealthy lover of his, but based on how Jeff described him, I expected to meet some kind of spiritual giant, a meditation guru who loved my friend.

Kaje had long been living a double life of his own. He had a wife in Redwood Shores who worked as the head nurse of Chope Community Hospital in San Mateo. They'd been married for twenty-eight years and had children and grandchildren together. Monday through Friday, Kaje lived in the city, ostensibly working his real estate business, while also carrying on with Jeff. On the weekends, he rejoined his wife in South Bay.

Kaje and Jeff picked me up in Kaje's black Mercedes, and we went to eat at the Squire Room in the Fairmont Hotel, one of the fanciest places I'd ever been to. I dressed in my old Charles Schwab attire, and Kaje brought me a sports jacket to complete the ensemble. Throughout the meal, Kaje kept complimenting me and telling me how attractive I was. Jeff, who was delusional even sober, was stoned out of his mind, so this flirtation didn't seem to bother him at all.

After dinner, we went to Kaje's two-bedroom, two-bathroom penthouse overlooking the Palace of Fine Arts, and all I kept thinking was, *I want to move in here.*

Given that I repeatedly failed to pay rent on Sycamore Alley—all of my escort money was spent on drugs—I soon got kicked out. I called Jeff to break the news.

"Well, you can come over here and stay," he said.

Living in close proximity, Kaje made advances, and I soaked it all up. Not long after I moved in, Jeff and Kaje broke up. Jeff had paranoid schizophrenia, and Kaje had lost patience with trying to control him during his breakdowns. What's more, Jeff had placed ads in the BAR and was turning tricks behind Kaje's back, while Kaje wanted more honesty and commitment. After they broke up, Jeff returned to a hot-line hotel on Polk Street, funded by disability payments.

Naturally, I stuck around—I wasn't about to let a good thing go to waste. I had this knack for attaching myself to men who could take care of me because I couldn't take care of myself—I had zero self-esteem, zero self-worth. I was just flying by the seat of my pants.

One of the things that attracted me to Kaje was how spiritual and into meditation he was, but little did I know that he would also supply me with plentiful amounts of speed. He reconciled his drug use with his spirituality by convincing himself he had total control over it. But he only appeared successful in comparison to me, a profoundly hopeless drug addict. We settled into a routine where he stayed home with me, shooting up copious amounts of meth Monday through Friday, and then he went home to his wife on the weekends. We became full-on, no-holds-barred, on-again-off-again speed freaks.

When I moved in, I told Kaje I wouldn't stop escorting: "I will be with you, and I'll always be here for you, but you can't make me give up my work." Because I stood my ground, he conceded. He turned one of the bedrooms into a total sex den that I could use with clients—he outfitted it with gear from Mr. S Leather, like leather vests and chaps, riding crops and floggers. He hung a leather sling from the ceiling and put up a tool-kit peg board on the wall to hold all kinds of toys and equipment. I rarely used any of this stuff; more often than not, I sold it off to buy drugs on the weekends when he'd gone home to his wife.

Even though Kaje provided speed all week long, when he went home, he was done. I was never done because I was an addict. When you're strung out on methamphetamine, the drug calls to you, and you will stop at nothing to get it. The high is so empowering, it makes you feel like you can do anything. You live in a delusion that everything is okay, even if you're living in a dumpster full of garbage. You believe the drug is working for you, when in fact it's not at all.

It was only a matter of weeks after first trying crystal meth that I also started trying to quit. Kaje and I would stop for a couple of weeks—we meditated, or we read from Tibetan Buddhist texts and discussed our ideas about spirituality and the nature of the Self. But somehow, I managed to steer us back to getting high again, and we resumed using until the wheels fell off. I was filled with so much self-loathing that nothing mattered. I didn't want to live in my body or feel any feelings or be where I was. I lived in this limbo between not wanting to live and not wanting to die, simply suspended in oblivion. Even in the worst of times, I always wanted to live. I wanted to feel alive, to be present and part of this planet, to be here, maybe not feeling feelings, but here. I didn't want to kill myself, or else they would win, whoever *they* were. The darkness would win. That was the idea: I'll never kill myself, and I'll never die. I'll outlive all of you motherfuckers. I'll show *you*.

When things got particularly rough, Kaje gave me two choices: go to detox or get the hell out. Our relationship became so volatile that he rented me an apartment on Eddy

Street in the Tenderloin so I'd have somewhere to go when he kicked me out, though eventually he stopped paying rent and I ended up on the streets again, homeless or living in some flophouse.

At one point, Edmund wanted me back. As tempted as I was to have a safe, stable home, I came clean to him. "I can't. I'm a drug addict, and I will never not be a drug addict, and I'll probably die a drug addict." I felt awful telling him what I'd become.

I started having paranoid, psychotic episodes, especially when I was on my own. Once, I was convinced religious zealots from the Christian Right were trying to oppress me—visions of crazed crowds plotted and planned to out me and shame me for my addiction. Another time, while walking down a street somewhere after dark, I thought the Chinese mafia were trailing me in sleek black cars. I started running, my chest tight and my breathing shallow. The cars sped up, so I sped up. I darted in and out of stores, getting stares from shoppers picking up prescriptions, toothpaste, or a roll of toilet paper. I dodged in and out of alleys, tripping over garbage cans. The delusion refused to fade until daybreak, when I had come down and the sun came up and I could make some sense of the world again.

And yet the insanity continued. Long before California declared a state of emergency for public health, needle exchange was unheard of. From time to time, I came across a man and a woman pushing a stroller through Civic Center Plaza, posing as a family. They were illegally trading dirty needles for clean ones—the first needle exchange in the nation. I was too afraid to approach them—it was still too high risk.

Sometimes I bought needles from homeless people on the street. They understood my needs, and their dirty rigs were my salvation. They also gave me a matchbook so I could sharpen the dull needle on the striker pad and maybe a bit of vodka or rubbing alcohol or a small vial of bleach to clean it. This ritual was always steeped in fear and loathing—contracting AIDS from sharing needles was just as common, if not more so, than getting it from sex. This was how I would die for sure.

Out of my mind, I shot up random drugs from any old stranger. I often ended up dope-sick in those days—fevers, sweats, and shakes took over my body. I would find myself curled up in some random hotel bathroom wishing for an end to the insanity. And yet I returned again and again to the needle and the thirty seconds of bliss at the end of the plunge. The feeling of wholeness, invincibility, a momentary escape from my brokenness and self-hatred. For a few minutes at a time, I didn't have to be me anymore. Those few minutes faded to seconds, and eventually the drugs gave me only a dash of normalcy at a time. This veil of delusion went on for decades. I truly believed that if I just got another hit, everything would be okay.

Sometime in 1991, I had an anxiety attack and thought I was losing my mind. Every little thing upset me—if the doorbell buzzed or a car alarm sounded, I nearly jumped out of my skin. I called a crisis hotline, and a woman named Antigone listened to me while I broke down.

"I need help. I'm strung out, and I don't know what to do. I feel like I'm losing my mind." At certain points, in hysterics, I swore to her I was dying—I just knew it.

She listened intently. She didn't judge me or attack my sense of reality. She occasionally asked things like, "When's the last time you got loaded? When do you think you'll get loaded again?" Her voice was calm and even.

Most importantly, she listened. She responded many times by saying, "Yes, I hear you. I believe you. It's going to be okay."

When I finished unloading on her, she switched gears into a more professional mode, giving my exhausted mind some direction. "Listen, I'm going to invite you to come to San Francisco General to meet with a woman named Bonnie Schwartz, an addiction case manager." Antigone gave me the hospital floor number and Bonnie's office number. "She'll be there today waiting for you."

I felt heard! Someone was there for me. Being the ever-irresponsible addict that I was, I nearly sabotaged this chance at a new life. I waited until well after five o'clock that evening before I mustered the courage to leave my apartment and trek to the hospital. Somewhere in the back of my mind, I wanted to say, *I showed up, but nobody was there.*

My subconscious plan was thwarted. Bonnie had waited for me, an amazing, incredible person who never abandoned me in all the years I stayed mired in addiction. Even as she changed jobs and hospitals, she kept me as her client for years and years. She was patient with me from the first day I met her. Sitting behind her desk, she asked me what I thought I needed. I just looked down at the floor, defeated and afraid.

"I don't know," I said. "I'm going to die anyway."

I probably had AIDS, and I doubted I'd ever escape this insanity of not wanting to live but not wanting to die. I was stuck in a limbo most drug addicts endure every day if they can't get clean.

Bonnie was matter-of-fact but compassionate. "You can go to treatment, or you can get loaded again. If you wait until you're ready, you might die before that day ever comes. Don't wait a lifetime to be ready."

On her recommendation, I went to my first 12-step meeting, Narcotics Anonymous, at a former record store on Market Street. I listened to the sobs of a heroin addict who had relapsed and felt that no one had supported her. I cried throughout the entire meeting, for her sense of betrayal, for the sadness of it all, for the weight of the world each person seemed to carry.

That was only the beginning of endless attempts and failures to get clean and stay clean. For years, I went to what seemed like every detox, treatment center, and hospital in California. Once, I even checked myself into a psych ward overnight. Desperate to stop using, I saw these people in recovery, living life, successful and happy. They had it all together. I wanted so badly to have what they had—just some semblance of peace. Still, there was always the pull to start using again. As soon as I'd detoxed and gotten some sleep, once the desperation had abated and I'd been clean for a while, with a general assistance check, food stamps, or some cash in my pocket, the ticker tape of my own ideas started rolling again: *This time it'll be different. This time I can manage it—I can do better.* Or I thought, *Fuck it. I don't care if it works or not. I need it.* Crystal meth called to me. Nothing could stand between us. I believed if I didn't get high, I was going to die. (Of what, I have no idea.)

And just like that, I was back on the needle.

Every time I got loaded, I thought, *I never want to do that again.* But then I would. Over and over. For a very long time, I lived in this existence where I would use and then go into a paranoid psychosis. After I came down, I felt remorseful and fell into a horrible, dreadful depression. *I never want to get loaded again. I want to get clean.* I'd try to get clean for a couple of weeks, and then lo and behold, I'd get high again. Each time the feelings were worse, the consequences more severe.

Around the time I met Bonnie Schwartz, Kaje got sick. He had contracted HIV from the partner he'd dated before Jeff, and by 1990, he had full-blown AIDS. He had Kaposi's sarcoma, the purple, cancerous skin lesions typical in AIDS patients, and he was put on a TPN, an intravenous feeding tube shunted into his chest, which he carried around in a backpack. I accompanied him from doctor to doctor for a series of treatments, but eventually he had to move back in with his wife, who learned about his double life in the worst way possible. He and I had been together on and off for four years by then, and he'd even come out to his family because he loved me so much. Knowing he would die soon, Kaje rented me a studio on Gough and Bush furnished with a number of his belongings. The studio was cheap and gorgeous, but I couldn't afford to pay the rent.

Around 1993, Kaje finally succumbed to AIDS.

During the time Kaje was dying, I was maintaining my usage. Somehow, I had begun a strict regimen of a half gram of meth a day—a quarter in the morning and a quarter at night—in order to have some semblance of normalcy. But there was nothing normal about my life.

Donnie, David, Linda, Gary, and Shari, 1969

Shari, Donnie, and me as Innocent David, 1971

Shari, my stepsiblings Lurlene and Trevor, and me as Broken David, 1974

First grade, 1974

At Ric West's house shortly after Kaje died, 1993

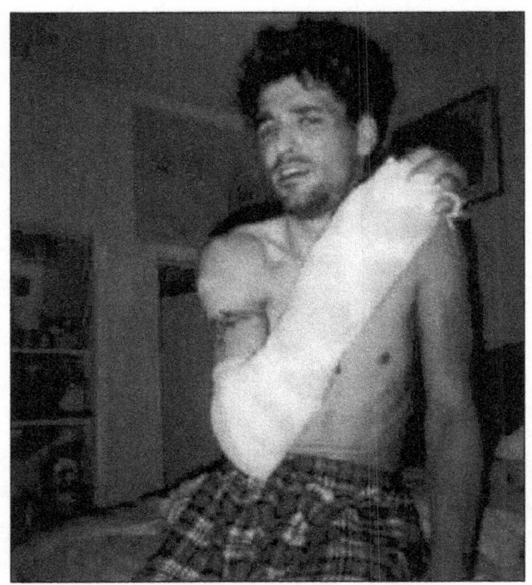

After the motorcycle accident, I had surgery following the removal of the two casts, January 2000

My beloved Bob just before starting David's Daily Dog Walks, Bernal Heights Park, 2005

David's Daily Dog Walks
Photo credit: Mike Kane, San Francisco Chronicle

Escort of the Year photo shoot, 2008
Photo courtesy of Barry Muniz

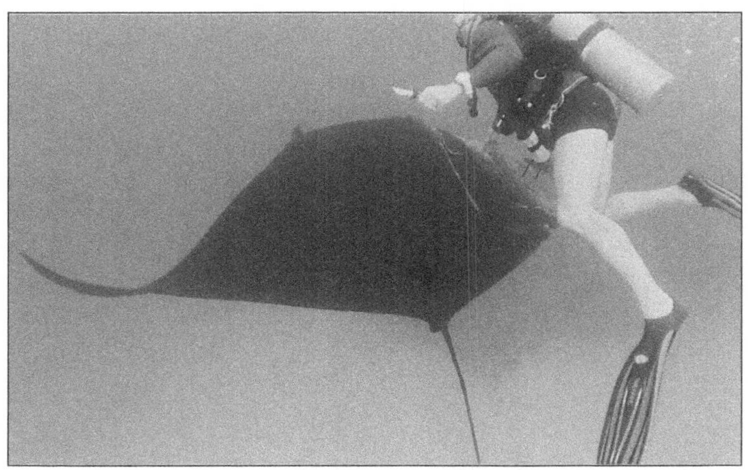

Dive master cutting the rope from the black manta ray,
Puerto Vallarta, Mexico, 2014

Walking with rescued elephants, Elephant Nature Park, Chiang Mai, Thailand, 2015

During the monthlong Male Adventure trip to Antarctica, 2016

Swimming with wild dolphins, Socorro Islands, Mexico, 2016

The sculpture of the little boy at MUSA, Cancún, Mexico, 2017

David, Todd, and Carl celebrating our seventh and final anniversary as a triad, Mexico, 2018

Taking a selfie with students from the Bwindi Plus Nursery and Primary School, Bwindi, Uganda, 2018

At the equator in Uganda, 2018

Communing with Silverback gorillas in Bwindi National Park, Uganda, 2018

Diving the Southern Red Sea, Egypt, 2019
Photo courtesy of Simon Lorenz

David and Marianne Williamson, Mindvalley A-Fest Reunion, March 2019

In loving memory of Shari Lynn Wagoner, March 12, 2019

CHAPTER 11

Just weeks before Kaje died, another drug addict friend of mine introduced me to a handsome guy named Ric West, who was thirty days sober. Ric came to visit me one day wearing leather pants laced up the side and a white fluffy pirate shirt.

"You're not really wearing that, are you?" I asked. "You're not getting in my pants wearing a pirate shirt."

He was out of that pirate outfit in no time! We started dating, and eventually, I moved into Ric's house in Glen Park. I fell head over heels in love with him. We stayed together for many years, but neither of us stayed clean for long. Sometimes we wouldn't have enough money for food because we'd spent it all on speed. Once, we stacked cardboard in the back of our pickup truck to sell to recycling—one hustle after another to stay high. We rode a roller coaster of getting loaded and then struggling to get clean and sober the entire time.

I kept seeking out help from Bonnie Schwartz. With no money or health insurance, one of the first programs she checked me into was a free twenty-eight-day facility called Tom Smith Detox at San Francisco General Hospital. I found myself at Tom Smith Detox numerous times before it ran out of funding and closed down. Another one was Palm Avenue Detox in San Mateo, which took patients on a sliding-scale basis. But once I'd been clean long enough to have some money and stability again, I went right back to the needle.

Sometime in 1996, my old friend Teresa convinced me to check into a program called Asian American Recovery Services, where she'd spent thirty-six months in treatment. She called me shortly before she graduated. "I'm clean and staying clean. You need to come here." She and I had been close for a long time, especially during those early years on the streets. If this program had worked for her, perhaps it could work for me, too. I had no place else to go. Ric had been forced to sell his house in Glen Park because of his addiction. We moved into an apartment building on High Street that his mother owned, but she promptly evicted us as well.

A hard-core program, AARS took in convicts facing extortion and murder charges and hope-to-die addicts who needed severe intervention. Nearly everyone had a court mandate to be there for sixteen months or else go to prison for a year. Snitches hiding out from their former Asian gangs knew they'd get whacked behind bars, so they went to treatment instead. And then there I was, voluntarily, a skinny white gay tweaker filling one of the beds reserved for outside demographics.

Two-story dorms held around thirty people, one for men and another for women, all in different places in their recovery. When I first arrived, I wasn't allowed any communication with the outside world for the first sixty days—no phone calls, no letters, no homing pigeons, no smoke signals from afar. After that, I was allowed one call a week to someone on the outside to let them know I was okay, but I had no one to call besides Ric. As a result, these gangbangers and dope fiends became my *de facto* family.

In process groups, we sat for hours in a circle of chairs in this large room with a white-tiled floor, hashing out the unfolding of our disease, relapse prevention, and people's behaviors. The counselors' primary approach was attack therapy. If someone screwed up, or if an old, unacceptable behavior pattern reemerged, the therapists sat that person in the middle of the room and just started screaming, "Who the fuck do you think you are? You're just a fucking loser, and you're going to destroy this whole family. Why don't you just take your ass out of here if you think you can do better on your own?"

The goal was to break down egos and build people back up according to the mores of the group: "You were a piece of shit when you got here, and you'll never be more than a piece of shit unless you do the work we tell you to do." That way of thinking worked well enough for the hardened and brutalized gangbangers who knew no other language, but other people ended up traumatized in such a community, their recovery based on shame-inducing invective, a tone and message they then carried and passed on to others as their own message to the world.

Outside of group, we were expected to follow a severe set of rules. If someone broke one of those rules, like leaving a pen on the table after a session, the counselors made everyone get out of bed and surround that pen on the table until the culprit owned up to the fact that they'd left it behind. Consequences ranged from cleaning the kitchen for a week or being ostracized to a bench for a day and denied any interaction with the rest of the group, except for meals and bedtime. Every tactic was about breaking you down to build you back up.

Teresa told me this program would change my life. She came back from time to time to participate in process groups and go nuts on everybody. "What the fuck is going on in this house?" she screamed. "Someone is keeping a secret, and you better come clean now because this house is loose!" After a heavy silence, someone would admit to something they'd done wrong or discuss their problem *du jour*. "I knew it," she'd say. "Who the fuck do you think you are? Everybody in the house is sitting here because you are fucked up."

I really believed I needed the intense chaos to get clean and sober. I thought if this worked for Teresa, a complete disaster, chances are it would work for me. Ironically, Teresa didn't stay sober—she started using heroin again and eventually died in 2004 from liver failure caused by hepatitis C.

After four months at AARS, I got kicked out for breaking a pencil in a fit of anger during a process group. An act of violence, they called it. One of the counselors said, "You can leave, or you can be on a ghost contract for seven days, where you'll clean and do manual labor, but you can't talk to anyone and no one can talk to you." At that point, I'd had it. I called Ric to come pick me up.

We stayed in a hotel on Lombard Street for a night or two until I could check into a ninety-day program at a treatment center called Walden House. I'd been to countless different facilities by this point, including four or five stays at Walden House already, though their ninety-day program was new, and they took a more holistic approach using acupuncture and massage. Their process groups were more focused on prevention and life skills and seemed more loving. *I can do this. If I can get through this program, I can get through anything.*

I met my first sponsor, a Native American named Johnnie Land, when he came to facilitate a 12-step meeting at Walden House. He sponsored me through the first four steps of the 12-step program, from admitting my own powerlessness to trusting in a higher power and turning over my life to its care. We were supposed to meet regularly, but he fell sick, and I didn't hear from him for a month or so.

When I went to visit him, I realized he had AIDS.

"You're gonna have to find a new sponsor," he said. "I'm getting sicker by the minute."

"No, I'll just wait until you get better, and we can finish working the steps."

A few days later, he was in a coma at San Francisco General Hospital, about a mile away from Walden House. I walked into his room to see him hooked up to a ventilator. His stomach was distended and his skin was yellowed with jaundice. Some other guys from the program circled his bed, holding vigil every day. Johnnie's dad, an attorney and medicine man, was present, along with his stepmother. We prayed for him and talked to him, hoping he could hear us, telling him we loved him and that it was okay for him to go.

But then three days later, he woke up. After the nurses removed his breathing tube, he kept saying, "I'm so thirsty!" Hospital staff had given us strict orders not to give him anything besides the occasional shave of ice, but how do you refuse a dying man? I ran to the store and bought a box of multiflavored popsicles. He devoured a few, and before I knew it, he had hurled an icy rainbow across the room.

His friends and family took turns holding him and telling him how much they loved him. It seemed he'd come out of his coma just to say goodbye. A few nights later, he passed away in his sleep.

I'd recently finished the fourth step, writing out "a searching and fearless moral inventory" of myself, the disaster that was my life scrawled out on sheets of notebook paper. The next step was to read it to another human being, but Johnnie died before we got that far. By the time he passed away, I'd graduated from the ninety-day program at Walden House and moved into a halfway house. His death shook me up, and I kind of lost my mind for a bit.

Around this time, I met my best friend Chris Freeman. We shared a love of all things Stevie Nicks. Over the years, we traveled the bumpy road of recovery together, each of us falling and getting back up numerous times. Chris was a joy to be around. Even when things were falling apart, he found a way to bring laughter into the room. By the end of his battle with AIDS, Chris died in hospice care, sober. His death hit me the hardest. He was such a light, and when he passed away, he left a hole in the world of all things joyful and crazy.

True to my intention, I stayed close to other friends who were dying of AIDS, like Brian, a using buddy and hope-to-die drug addict I knew from a transaction at a crack house, a guy who happened to be the sweetest, most caring person I knew. He told me, "I'm never going to stop using." He died in a hospital of full-blown AIDS at twenty years old.

Another friend, Steve, a vibrant, gentle soul with ocular toxoplasmosis as a result of HIV, was deteriorating in hospice. He didn't want to be alone, so I pushed him in his wheelchair to the movie theater, doing wheelies on the handicap ramps and laughing the entire time. He farted up a storm in the theater, but we simply laughed it off. "Uh, oh. Oh well, what are they going to do, kick us out?"

Before I knew it, he was gone, too.

In 1996, the cocktail HAART (highly active antiretroviral therapy) hit the market, but it took us a long time to realize that people were getting better. People were still dying left and right. Those experiences ripped a hole in my soul. I spent so many moments in sober spaces, meeting houses, and hospital rooms watching my friends die. *Here we are again, sitting vigil.* I could never get my head around it or accept it. It felt so unfair. I kept thinking, *This recovery thing has too many feelings. I'm not going to make it.* The grief was unbearable.

But somehow, I managed to stay sober, at least for a

When I finally achieved my first year of sobriety, I bro up with Ric West. I'd been told not to make any major changes in the first year of recovery, so I waited to end it, even though I knew I needed to be on my own for a while. Our relationship wasn't working because my relationship with myself wasn't working. I needed to be single. I needed to get to know me. My entire life had been an endless dependency on a person or a drug or a system. I needed to not be taken care of by someone else for once.

Sometime in mid-1998, while living at the halfway house, I discovered financial advisor Suze Orman on the *Oprah Winfrey Show*. In 1997, Orman had published her second book, *The Nine Steps to Financial Freedom: Practical and Spiritual Steps So You Can Stop Worrying*. After a brief initial appearance on *Oprah* earlier in 1998, Orman went on to appear on Oprah's show at least fourteen more times to talk about that one book alone.

During one of those episodes, something she said changed my life. I was sitting in the common area watching TV when Orman addressed the camera. "We're going to take a commercial break, but when we get back, I'm going to show you the one and only perfect way to have as much money and success in your life as you'll ever need. Grab a pen and a piece of paper and stay tuned."

Intrigued and with nothing to lose, I found a pen and some paper and waited for the show to return.

Back on set, Orman told the story of how she had been defrauded of an investment by an unscrupulous trader at Merrill Lynch only to then go work for the financial firm herself. Scared stiff of whether or not she could succeed in the investment business, she began repeating an affirmation:

l, and successful, producing at least ten
›nth." She explained how she wrote this
ıty-five times a day and repeated it to
positive truth to replace the fear and
ılity.

ge you to do the same thing," she said. "I want you to think of an amount of money you want to make every month. Keep your statement simple and in the present tense."

I wrote down something really easy: "I'm happy and healthy, and I make at least ten thousand dollars a month." I figured if that's how she started out, I might as well emulate her efforts.

Then she said, "I want you to write down your affirmation twenty-five times a day. Say it to yourself when you're brushing your teeth or riding up an elevator and before you go to bed at night. Every time you're afraid, replace your fear with your positive message."

For three weeks, I followed her instructions religiously. I wrote down and repeated my affirmation twenty-five times a day and every night before I went to bed. I embodied my desire to be happy, healthy, and prosperous, and I began to believe that I could truly attract a better life outside of the halfway house.

And that's when things started to shift.

I was walking down Van Ness Avenue one afternoon when I saw a gigantic sign that said, "Now Hiring! New Chevy's Fresh Mex, 590 Van Ness." Wearing just my street clothes and unprepared for an interview, I walked across the street to apply. A young woman named Stacey said, "You look like you'd be a perfect fit." She hired me on the spot before I'd even finished filling out the application.

Soon, I was Chevy's number one waiter—I received the best shifts and the best stations and the highest sales night after night. Every evening after my shift, I stuffed handfuls of cash into an old circuit breaker box on the wall of my room until I could no longer close the door. With this new influx of cash, I moved into an apartment just two blocks away from the restaurant, and I bought a motorcycle—all kinds of hot guys wanted to ride on the back of my bike!

My life had taken off. I wasn't making anywhere close to ten thousand dollars a month, but I had more equity in living than I'd had in decades on the street. Just as Jeff Stevenson had taught me all those years earlier, I saw how I could truly manifest and create my own life. Immersed in a raw form of gratitude, I couldn't help thinking, *Oh my God, I survived! I'm clean and sober. I'm not digging into a trash can or sticking a needle into my arm.* Every day, a laundry list of joys flooded my mind.

But I also couldn't help thinking other things, like, *This is bullshit. This can't last. I don't deserve any of this.* Some broken part of my being refused to let me be. I stopped writing and repeating my affirmations. I stopped manifesting. I quit going to meetings, which I justified to myself because no one in those meetings was staying clean anyway. My focus shifted.

And that's when everything fell apart.

CHAPTER 12

In 1998, after I'd had about fifteen months of sobriety, I planned a late-summer trip to Mexico. I had fallen into a deep depression, and I hoped getting away might help. From the first day of sobriety, I still felt totally miserable living in my skin. I was glad for a reprieve from addiction, and though I didn't want to go back to what I knew was horrible, I had no escape from the self-loathing. I didn't want to live anymore, and yet I didn't want to die either.

Throughout that time in recovery, I kept thinking something was wrong with me, but I didn't know what it was. I tried everything to avoid this feeling of wrongness—I had all kinds of sex, I worked a lot, I smoked nonstop. Cigarette burns dotted my apartment floor because I would wake up in the middle of the night and light up, only to fall asleep and drop the cigarette. It's a miracle I didn't burn the place down and kill myself in the blaze.

I'd grown tired of sitting in Narcotics Anonymous meetings with these horrifying basket cases I thought were such losers. *Don't they know none of this stuff really works?* They kept talking about this God thing, but the God I knew from Catholic catechism and my parents' example was harsh and punishing, and I could only earn his love by being good, which was hopeless, because as far as I was concerned, I was irreparably broken. I finally got to the point where I was saying to myself, "Fuck God. Fuck this program. Fuck all of you people talking about love because none of this is real. What's real is the fact that I need to get loaded every single day for the rest of my life so that I don't have to feel anymore. Because if I have to feel, I'm going to die. I'm going to kill myself. I can't keep living with this horrific pain and self-hatred."

So, I stopped going to meetings and doing the work to stay sober. I figured I was special and could make things work on my own. I decided I was tired from working so much, and now that I had some money, I wanted to take a two-week vacation and travel to a foreign country like I'd dreamed of as a kid. A friend in recovery, a slim, short-haired Latina named Lani, agreed to travel with me for the first week of my trip. We flew to Mérida, the capital of Yucatán and the farthest northern city in the Yucatán Peninsula below Progreso, the beach town with a Mexican Navy base. We spent the next week on *colectivos*, small transport vans, headed toward Cancún, stopping along the way to backpack through the Yucatán jungles and visit Mayan ruins such as Uxmal, Chichen Itza, and Puuc Route.

From Cancún, we took a ferry to Isla Mujeres, an island off of the eastern coast, and rented a room in a hostel. Despite the natural wonder, the depression I'd hoped to shake off still clung to me. I stayed stuck and encapsulated inside my head. I couldn't understand why I felt so despondent when I had such a seemingly fabulous life. I'd flown to the farthest part of Mexico and backpacked into the depths of the jungle, and yet I still couldn't escape myself. I couldn't get away from how much I hated being in my body.

I couldn't wait for Lani to leave so I could finally get drunk.

After a week, Lani flew home from Cancún, and I stayed on Isla Mujeres, feeling horribly lonely once she left. I wrote her a postcard that said, "I miss you. And it's very lonely here. I hope by the time you get this, all will have changed. I am deep within myself and feel very lonely. I know this was not the plan. I'm staying on Isla till I meet some people, I hope. Love you, David."

It would take weeks before that postcard reached her.

A few days after Lani left, I found myself at a palapa that sold drinks and tacos on the beach. I fed scraps to the street dogs and stared across the sand to the waves lapping the shore. There on the beach, feeling alone and empty, I took a sip of a margarita.

That was the beginning of the end.

Nothing else in the world could have eased that inner torment or cured my emptiness besides that toxin on ice. Nothing else could begin to blot out my sense of brokenness and separation or fill the void I felt within. Even in the short recovery I'd accomplished so far, I had been living in a prison of my own making with no real intimacy with others or any sense of interconnectedness. I felt desperate for relief—I needed oblivion to blot out the pain.

I drank all the way through Mexico until I couldn't drink another drop. After I left Isle Mujeres, I met a blonde girl and her sister from Australia on a bus. I don't remember where I was going, but a man was standing on the side of a road with a howler monkey in hand, taking money from tourists who wanted to pet it. The Australian girl, moved with compassion for this tortured animal, flew out the door and confronted him: "Let the monkey go, now!" I was so enamored by her bravery, I quickly befriended her and her sister. We took a *colectivo* six hundred miles to Bonampak, a Mayan ruin in Chiapas near the Guatemalan border, and then on to Yaxchilan and Palenque.

In Palenque, we drank mushroom tea, an eye-opening psychedelic trip. My new Aussie friend explained that these ruins were once a university. As we walked around the structures, she shared ideas that made complete sense to me in that state of mind. She loved to speculate that alien life forms had taught the Mayans math and science and how to build these structures. She even believed the Mayans were abducted to another planet after predicting our future demise.

In southern Mexico, somewhere in the Lacandón Jungle, we swam in the waters of a local cenote, an underground limestone cave where fresh-water runoff collected into pools. We were surrounded by lush rain forest and the sounds of howler monkeys. The three of us provided a buffet of blood for swarms of fleas and mosquitos, and I ended up with dengue fever, though I didn't realize what it was at the time. Sick as sick could be, I pounded Aleve and Imodium to ward off the symptoms.

I needed to get home—I was sick out of my mind—so my travel companions and I parted ways. Despite being desperately ill, I made it my mission to get high as soon as possible. The adventure I'd longed for was now merely an obstacle to using drugs. I changed my flight to an earlier return home and hopped on a bus to the closest airport.

After my flight landed in San Francisco, I went home to drop off my bags, and then I headed out to find Jacob, a former drug buddy who had also lived with me at the halfway house. He was both my friend and my arch nemesis, the bane of my existence. I hated him when we were shooting up together, and I hated him when we were trying to get clean. I couldn't figure out why I detested him so badly, but in hindsight, I think it's because I saw so much of myself in him, the neediness and attention seeking and chronic dependency. We had a love-hate relationship; in drug addiction, you keep your enemies close and develop these bizarre relationships because they might rob you or kill you at any moment. But I knew I could count on him, and I knew he had already relapsed himself.

"How quickly can you get me some meth?" I asked.

"No way, David. I'm not going to be that guy," he said.

"Well, just so you know, I've already used. So, you're not that guy. I'm that guy."

Jacob reluctantly agreed. The next thing I knew, I was plunging a needle into my arm and melting into oblivion.

Though I'd wasted down to 110 pounds, I remained clueless about the nature of my illness. I called my ex Ric West for help. "I think there's something really wrong with me."

When he walked in, he took one look at my green skin and skeletal frame and said, "I'm calling an ambulance."

Ric told the paramedics I'd recently been to Mexico and must have picked up some kind of bug, perhaps giardiasis, so they showed up wearing hazmat suits and pushing a wheelchair instead of a gurney. I couldn't blame them—I looked like an alien.

"We don't mean to scare you or offend you," the paramedics explained, "but we don't know what you might have brought back."

Hospital tests revealed dengue fever, a viral infection with few treatment options besides fluids and pain relievers. I spent what felt like weeks in the hospital. The illness stressed my immune system so that I broke out in shingles, and cold sores lined my mouth.

Ever my cheerleader, Ric visited me regularly. "I can't believe you're even alive," he said.

At the end of August, the hospital released me, or what was left of me, and the first thing I did was drag my skin and bones to the Nob Hill Theatre, the only all-male strip club in San

Francisco, to meet up with a friend and his drug dealer. I took the drug dealer home with me and stayed high for I don't even know how long.

Marginally better and still strung out, I started picking up shifts at Chevy's again. I didn't want anyone to know I was shooting up speed, so I took downers like Ativan and Valium, which then made me slur my words or fall asleep standing up. No longer their best waiter, I skipped a scheduled shift and promptly lost my job.

High on speed and tranquilizers, I called Ron Castner at the Walden House detox facility. "I need to come in," I said. "I'm going to die out here."

"Okay, come on down. We have a bed for you."

I walked in to start yet another detox, which might have unfolded normally if I hadn't been on all those benzodiazepines, which typically require medical supervision, especially given the amount I'd been using. But I didn't know that. Lying in bed, a whoosh of movement swirled in my skull, a disorienting vertigo that left me unable to sit up or stand or focus.

Walden House staff offered me tea and water and encouraged me to stick it out. "Stay in bed, and you'll get through this." But after three days, I couldn't tolerate the dizzying head rush a moment longer. The only solution was to leave. As I hightailed it out of the facility, Ron ran after me. He had never run after a client before to ask them to stay. He probably realized I was detoxing from something different, but they'd missed it. Everyone assumed I was a speed freak—they had no idea I'd been taking Ativan and Valium, too.

"I'll come back when I'm feeling better," I called out, "but I can't stay here anymore."

As soon as I arrived at the little studio that I'd rented just months earlier, I made a phone call. A hit of meth, the head rush cleared, and I felt better. And in that moment, I lost all hope.

I'm never going to get clean, I told myself. *It's never going to happen—there's just no way. I'm just different, and nothing works for me. This is it.*

Surrendered to the drug, I now had to find a better way to use. I couldn't remain a hope-to-die drug addict anymore—I had to find a way to make it work so I didn't end up homeless on the streets again. Once I'd given up on getting clean, all my paranoia evaporated. I felt fearless. I resolved to do whatever it took.

Little by little, I sold off everything I had acquired during the year and a half of sobriety—brand-new CDs, including my entire Stevie Nicks collection, and most of the clothes in my closet. Once I ran out of things to sell, I started dealing drugs instead, just small amounts to support my habit.

In September 1998, I turned thirty years old. On Thanksgiving Day, not long after I'd made the final payment on my motorcycle, a taxicab ran a red light and slammed into me. The crash totaled my bike and broke both my arms. The settlement from Yellow Cab wouldn't arrive until five years later.

One by one, every single thing I had worked for during recovery was destroyed.

I found myself surrounded by what the 12-step program calls "lower companions"—thieves and grifters and criminals of all kinds. Among them, I met my next partner, Richard Scott. His then-boyfriend, Peter, asked me to come over and help Richard—who was fresh out of a stint in prison for identity theft and counterfeiting—get loaded because he didn't know how to shoot himself up. I walked into this room in the

Haight-Ashbury to encounter a beautiful, thin, well-groomed young guy, the kind who might otherwise pull off a slick suit and tie. I shot him up, packed up my stuff, and left.

One day, Richard showed up at my apartment on Willow Street just off of Van Ness Avenue. "I need your help again," he said.

I was extremely attracted to him, so I had no qualms about letting him in. Richard and I got high together, and he spent the night. It would be an understatement to say Peter lost his mind—he went batshit crazy about my stealing his boyfriend. I feigned no innocence, but I couldn't help it. Despite being a complete disaster myself, I kept thinking, *Someone needs to take care of this poor guy besides that disaster boyfriend of his*. The two of them were about to be evicted from Peter's apartment anyway, so Richard needed somewhere to go. He secured a spot with me fairly quickly.

Richard became my partner for the next eight years, as well as my partner in crime. He was a sociopathic genius and too smart for his own good; he'd never had a job in his life but lived off one scam after another. After he moved in, he immediately ordered Dell desktop computers he'd purchased using someone else's identity and taught me how to use them, as well as how to navigate the burgeoning internet.

Soon, we were neck deep in sophisticated forms of white-collar crime to support our meth habit, things we'd never get away with today because internet security is so much more advanced. But back then, wireless internet had only just been released for consumers in 1997, and the earliest forms of encryption weren't around yet. By mid-1999, Napster offered the first known peer-to-peer file-sharing application, followed by BearShare in late 2000. But the music-sharing programs didn't only share music; when people dialed in and logged on to swap mp3s, they unwittingly exposed their entire hard drives.

Richard and I hacked people's hard drives and downloaded files full of personal information, tax and financial documents, and legal paperwork. We mined the internet for mountains of available data from unwitting software users whose identities we used to acquire computer equipment, clothing, and anything else we could buy online, which we then sold for drugs. It was a lot of work for very little because most of the time we didn't get away with it—somewhere along the way we got blocked by the retail store or computer company.

At one point, someone we knew had gone dumpster diving behind an industrial park and retrieved the remains of a computer server full of customer information from American Express, Saks Fifth Avenue, and a nearby hotel. The hard drive contained a wealth of files with customers' first and last names, credit cards, and Social Security numbers. We converted the information to text files and burned the profiles onto CDs to trade for drugs from criminally inclined acquaintances who stole identities, made fake IDs, and drafted hot checks.

This move proved to be our downfall. When law enforcement caught these guys, our names came up repeatedly as the guys who had provided the CDs. Without our knowing it, the United States Postal Inspection Service began building a case against us for mail fraud, wire fraud, and creating fraudulent IDs.

Because Richard was on probation, the police had a right to enter our place of residence at any time and search his belongings. On one particular occasion, SFPD raided our apartment. Three officers in uniform and a plainclothes detective pushed through the door. They sat us handcuffed in chairs while they gathered evidence, including a piece of transparency paper that had a printed hologram from a California driver's license, which we used to create fake identities for cashing hot checks, along with an airline ticket purchased with a stolen credit card. Sometime before the raid, in a fit of paranoia, I'd thrown away the hard drive with all of the personal profiles on them, but they found a few of the CD-ROMs we had burned.

Despite the fact that Richard was on probation, the officers left without making any arrests. Richard's assumption was that they left him alone because they were still building a case against us. We simply picked up where we left off, waiting to see how long we could get away with it. As it turned out, the hammer wouldn't fall for another five years.

Not long after Richard moved in with me, I saw him looking at images online of young puppies available for adoption. I was like, "No way dude. We are drug addicts. The last thing we need is a dog." But then one day, without telling me, he adopted a four-month-old blond pit bull named Bob from a local rescue group. The moment he put that dangly puppy in my lap, I knew I was forever that dog's prisoner. I started crying. "Okay, so we have a kid now." I was sold. There was no turning back.

Bob had been part of a litter of puppies rescued from a drug house after a police raid gone bad. When the momma dog tried to attack the officers, they shot and killed her, leaving her puppies traumatized. Bob had severe PTSD and cowered at everything; we couldn't put him on a leash and take him for a walk for the first three years of his life. Instead, we just carried him everywhere. But once we set him down in a park with other animals, he changed completely and played with the other dogs.

He was a sweet, submissive, beautiful, broken dog with an amazing spirit, the real witness to how bad things became for me during those first seven years of his life. Out of everyone I've ever hurt, Bob was the most innocent and least deserving of all the chaos I brought into our lives.

After we were evicted from our apartment on Willow Street for failure to pay rent, Richard and I were homeless and often separated. We lived on the streets or in flophouses. At one point, one of the drug dealers I knew told us we could crash on top of her building in Hayes Valley. Richard and I hauled Bob, who weighed eighty-five pounds, up a metal fire escape to the roof of an old Victorian that had an access door to a small circular terrace where we could sleep for a few nights. Later, we ended up in a seedy drug house on Folsom and Tenth, surrounded by eight other people all involved in various forms of fraud. Mounds of stolen property came in and out of that squalid house, which only heightened police scrutiny on our activities.

In the fall of 2004, after five years of legal wrangling, I finally received the settlement from Yellow Cab for the motorcycle accident. Out of the $150,000 award, I received $77,000, which lasted us a month, maybe two. Richard and I lived large, gambled, gave money away, spent a ton on drugs, lost what was left. Given that the feds were watching us, the sudden influx of money raised a red flag.

One night, we rented a room at a Holiday Inn near the Civic Center to get away from the chaos at the drug house. Richard had gone to visit his probation officer, and on his way back, five US Postal Inspectors trailed him to where we were staying. Once inside, the officers separated us. I was forced to lie face down on the carpet in the hallway while the officers peppered me with questions, but I just kept repeating, "I don't know what you're talking about." One officer started naming people they'd arrested and interrogated, people I'd sold CDs to, implying we were all part of some huge crime ring, which we weren't. They confiscated several money orders for $500 each—leftover money from my settlement—and my small Sony laptop, which contained reams of damaging information. The officers took Richard into custody but left me alone.

The files they found on my laptop matched the evidence they had in holding, and soon a judge had issued an arrest warrant for us both on charges of conspiracy to commit credit card fraud, possession of stolen mail, possession of five or more authentication features with intent to produce false ID, and other activities related to fraud. The total charges added up to fifty-five years in a federal penitentiary. For reasons I can't quite explain, Richard was released from custody a few hours later.

"They signed me out on a hundred-thousand-dollar signature bond with a promise to show up in court," he said. "You have to go down to the station and sign the bond, too."

Following the raid, we remained on supervised release, but as soon as my probation officer saw that we lived in a house full of criminals, there were soon warrants out for our arrest for violating the terms of our probation. When the officers showed up to arrest us, I wasn't there. Richard was taken into custody and agreed to enroll in a long-term drug treatment program while his case was being processed. The federal justice system has about a 93 percent conviction rate, which meant he would likely be found guilty of some charges, but the treatment program would demonstrate his desire to reform.

I knew they wanted me to turn myself in, but I didn't want to end up incarcerated. In case the worst happened, I needed to be sure someone took care of Bob while I was away. I asked my friend Bobby to meet me at Duboce Park, situated between

Duboce Triangle and Lower Haight. Bob loved to run and play, and Duboce Park had been a refuge for us, as well as a meeting point for Richard and me whenever we were separated on the streets—we knew one of us would eventually return to the park with Bob, so we could circle back and find each other there. When Bobby arrived, I was standing on a hill on the edge of the park, sobbing uncontrollably. I asked Bobby to take Bob with him to Livermore in Alameda County, where he'd recently secured a new place to live. He agreed, and I turned over my beloved dog to his care.

From there, I was off and running. I camped out with an old drug-dealer friend named John, sleeping on the floor of his flea-ridden hotline hotel room in the Tenderloin. Tweaked out of my mind, I had become that guy carrying garbage bags and screaming at trees, a strung-out disaster. My skin was dry and ashen, my teeth black and rotten. While I was staying with John, shingles broke out all over my body; the sores puffed and blistered and broke open, eventually hardening into a scab the size of two sheets of paper down the side of my body.

As soon as I was well enough to get out and carouse around, I left John's hotel. It was December 2004. Back along the Tenderloin track, I ran into a friend. "Hey, you wanna make a bit of cash?" he asked. "I could get you some drugs, and we'll split whatever money you make." He wrote me a hot check for two hundred dollars. "Go down to the Wells Fargo on Post and Powell. Cash this, and we'll each take a hundred."

He assured me the tellers wouldn't call on a check for two hundred dollars or less, so I folded it into my pocket and headed for the bank. I walked in unbathed and unshaven, weighing a whole buck twenty and grinding what little teeth I had left, delusional enough to think I was put together enough to pass a hot check to a banker.

I even set my real California driver's license down on the counter.

The teller glanced at my ID and gave me tight, thin smile. "No problem. I'll be right back—I just need to grab some extra cash."

"Never mind, I gotta go." I grabbed my ID and beelined for the exit. I sped-walked half a block down the street, right past the guy who had written me the fake check. "Get the fuck out of here," I hissed. He took off.

I hadn't traveled far before a cop car pulled up, followed immediately by two unmarked cars. A police officer jumped out and pointed his gun straight at me. "DON'T MOVE! DON'T MOVE!"

I stopped dead in my tracks. This was it. The jig was up.

I slowly raised my arms above my head, until the officer yanked my wrist and forced me to the ground. "You're under arrest for attempted robbery." As the side of my face pressed into the concrete, the sparkling grain reflecting bits of sunlight, I felt an overwhelming sense of relief. As crazy and wild-eyed as I was, I knew in this moment that I didn't have to run anymore. It was over.

I was processed in a local jail cell on some weird side alley off Powell Street before being loaded onto a transport bus to a federal hold at Santa Rita Jail in Dublin.

Given how sick I looked, prison staff took me straight to the infirmary. My spirit broken and my body temperature rising, the vinyl mattress became soaked and unbearable to lie on. I rolled off the gurney onto the cement floor, feeling the cool surface against my cheek. I felt myself surrender. *Please, God, help me. All I want is a chance to live through this. Something's got to give.*

In that instant, I knew my life was going to be different, but I couldn't at all foresee how.

CHAPTER 13

For the next nine months, I lived in a chronic state of uncertainty about my future.

During intake at the Santa Rita Jail, the deputy assigned me an inmate number and handed me a bed roll and a set of bright red clothing, which indicated I was in protective custody. The guys in my maximum-security pod included gay men, transgendered women, gang snitches, and others who wouldn't fare well in the barbarically violent general population.

When I arrived, the inmates in my pod were roaming around on their one hour of recreation for the day, watching television or playing cards or mingling with each other. One of them was this super-hot muscle daddy with tattoos all over his neck. As he walked over to me, I fantasized that this gorgeous gangbanger would take me under his wing and protect me from all the evil jail villains.

"Man, you look fucked up." He handed me a cup of hot chocolate mixed with coffee, something he'd purchased from the commissary, and let me finish it off. "Don't worry about it," he said.

By that point, I was jonesing so bad, coming down from meth and crack and whatever else in the A-to-Z suite of drugs I took. My whole body buzzed with a pain like that zing up your elbow when you slam your funny bone on the corner of a table. I felt so horrible I just crouched down and spread myself out across the cold concrete floor. I passed out right there while everyone else was dancing and making noise around me.

After the hour-long break was over, a trustee led me to a cell with this tiny little guy named James who had been accused of exposing himself to children at a bus stop. James later explained that he had been drinking and passed out in his car. When he opened the door to take a piss, a bunch of kids were standing at the bus stop, right there with his wang hanging out. The bus driver called the cops. An innocent mistake, he said. He was creepy, but he was mostly a harmless elfin. I didn't know the truth of the story, and I didn't want to know. When other guys tried to prod me into snooping for details, I just said, "The guy is a harmless hobbit from the shire. Leave him alone. It's sad."

Once I was successfully housed with the hobbit, I looked through the toiletry kit I'd been given at intake—a small sandwich bag containing a plastic travel toothbrush, a tiny vial of toothpaste, a plastic comb, and some body lotion. I took out the toothbrush and toothpaste and walked over to a square of scratched-up stainless steel on the wall that functioned as a mirror. As I moved the toothbrush back and forth, the enamel on my lower teeth just crumbled away, revealing more black decay. The deterioration was painless because my teeth were already dead. Staring at what was left of my mouth—just tiny slivers the color of charcoal—I started to cry. *This is what I've become. This is where I've gotten myself.*

Over the next several weeks, I continued to detox from drugs, alcohol, and nicotine—I slept most of the time, getting up occasionally to talk to guys across the hallway. I didn't socialize much at first until I met the half dozen transgendered inmates, girls like Tamica and Laylay who were in for armed robbery or mail theft or violating probation. On the outside, many of them worked the streets, profiting from the fetishes of men who like women who have penises, and on the inside, they ruled the roost with prison daddies for protection.

Besides the arraignment and initial court hearings for my case, I fell into a monotonous and seemingly endless mode of waiting. Day by day, week to week, month to month, I simply waited. With little word from the outside, I took up a letter-writing campaign to plea for mercy. I purchased paper, pencils, envelopes, and postage from the prison commissary using money from my public assistance checks. My settlement long spent, these precious checks were mailed each month to a check-cashing center owned by a Russian couple who took great pity on me and agreed to send me money to live on while I was incarcerated.

I wrote one letter after another, including countless missives to the judge on my case, Phyllis J. Hamilton, a no-nonsense district judge. I wrote to my congressional representatives, attorneys, probation officers, and even Joyce Meyers, the famous televangelist who runs the Hand of Hope prison ministry. Not a day went by that I didn't send a letter begging to be put in a drug program and declaring I was willing to go to any lengths to get the help I needed, if only someone would give me another chance. I would have written to Mr. Rogers and the pope, if I had thought it would help my case.

I had only two visitors the entire time I was in Santa Rita, in part because it's an incredibly long and complicated process to get cleared into the facility, and few people I knew were clean and straight enough to get past all the barriers. My partner, Richard, who had escaped from his drug treatment program the day I got arrested, sent an attorney to have me sign a power of attorney because Richard needed my public assistance checks. The attorney happened to be another junkie who had managed to maintain his license to practice. He let me know that Richard had our dog, Bob. That was all I needed to hear. I let him clean me out—hundreds of dollars that had piled up. He reneged on his promise to put three hundred dollars on my books, leaving me completely broke.

Being on the run, Richard couldn't even send me a letter, but from time to time, he managed to send word through a friend with an update on Bob's whereabouts. At first all was well, but then later I received another letter from a friend who said, "I don't know what to tell you about Bob, but Richard left him tied up outside on Tenth Street, and somebody went and picked him up. I'm sure they're taking better care of him than Richard was."

I feared all kinds of scenarios—maybe animal control captured Bob, or someone kidnapped him and turned him into a fight dog, in which case I was just certain he was being completely traumatized all over again.

Every night in my cell, lying in the bottom bunk bed listening to the hobbit's light snoring, I repeated the same prayers: "Dear God, please let me hold Richard in my arms for one more night, just to tell him I love him. Please let my dog be okay, and let me hold my dog again."

In maximum security, inmates usually spend twenty-three hours a day in their cells with time out to shower. The only exceptions to the schedule are breakfast and dinner (they delivered bag lunches to our cells), doctor or lawyer visits, court hearings, and Sunday church services. I had little reprieve from my destabilized existence, confined to this jail cell with the hobbit, who also happened to be a big-time Jesus freak. Our only interaction was when we read the Bible together or went to hear the evangelical pastor in the chapel on Sundays.

The pastor, a teddy bear of a white man about forty-five years old, alternated Sundays with a black Baptist preacher and two sisters—female ministers who assisted him. They played guitar, told stories, screened movies like *The Passion of the Christ*, and held many prayer circles. One time, my head was bowed in prayer when one of the sisters tapped me on the shoulder. "Baby, don't look down. Look up when you pray, or you might miss something! You never know what God has in store for you."

On Sundays, the trans girls and I often sat in the chapel cruising guys and goofing off. The pastor brought music for us to sing, and though I'm a horrible singer, some of the other inmates could belt their hearts out. One of the girls had a voice like Whitney Houston, and as I stood next to her, listening to the lyrics of "I Can Only Imagine" by MercyMe, her angelic voice seemed to usher us all into the presence of God. There we stood, in this tiny little room, a bunch of misfits—black, white, Asian, Hispanic, Arab—all of us ensnarled in our various self-made catastrophes. The vibration of the music, compounded by the close walls and metallic chairs, disarmed us, priming us for a spiritual experience.

I had a come-to-Jesus moment during my time in prison. In that place, I was constantly reminded of how we were still unforgiven and unforgivable, many of us still waiting to be sentenced for the crimes we'd committed. I lived in an institutionalized purgatory waiting on Judgment Day. With nothing else to think about, besides the fight for my life, I spent plenty of time ruminating on all my wrongness, my broken life of addiction. This was where my best thinking had gotten me.

As 12-step programs say, "No human power could have relieved us." My way evidently wasn't working, and I resolved to surrender to something greater.

That day, I took to heart the preacher's message of restoration and forgiveness, a pathway to redemption. And in that surrender, I looked up to pray, just like the sister had suggested. My experience was certainly different—I felt exposed and vulnerable. Suddenly, the presence of some sort of Christlike spirit entered my heart and showered over me. I felt overcome by love and relief. All of those illusory cracks and crevices that made me think I was so broken began to fade. I understood the concept of dying in order to live—I had to kill off all those old ideas that kept me trapped in a belief system about my own brokenness. I felt the sister grip my hand—she knew this was it. She smiled and gave me a look that said, "I told you so."

This beautiful experience of divine love opened my heart and mind to something more, a conscious acknowledgement that I was absolutely loved and lovable. *I'm going to be okay.* And I hadn't been okay for so long, not just years, but across the entire trajectory of my life. In that jailhouse church surrounded by those resounding harmonics and that ragtag group of convicts who believed they were going be okay too, relief and gratitude and tears poured out, and I let go into my first real sense of peace.

When I was still on the run from the cops, I went to the hospital to visit my arch nemesis and dear friend Jacob, who was dying of AIDS. Over the years, we had developed a connection, and I was one of the few people he trusted. He weighed little more than a hundred pounds and was hooked up to a feeding tube. Lying in his hospital bed, he confided in me: "I've made peace with myself and the fact that I'm dying. I'm tired of shitting my pants, I'm tired of not being able to swallow food, and I'm just tired. I want to go."

I was like, "Well, go then."

It was sad and heartbreaking because as much as I couldn't stand him, I always felt a sense of obligation to help him when he showed up at my door with his hand out—I gave him money or clothes or drugs—and he sometimes helped me when I needed help, albeit rarely. He represented so much I hated about myself and all the ways I behaved.

When I left the hospital, I broke down in tears. I assumed I'd just said goodbye to another friend lost to AIDS. Once I was arrested, I assumed Jacob was long dead and gone.

Months passed while I was in prison, until one day my ex-boyfriend Ric West came for a visit. He was the only person besides Richard's attorney who had come to see me. I sat down in a telephone cubicle, separated from my visitor by a thick pane of glass, and picked up the phone. Ric sat in the opposite chair with the phone against his ear, grinning. Then, Jacob walked up behind him—not only alive, to my great shock and amazement, but healthy, muscular, with a full and glowing face. He was a completely different person.

Jacob tapped on the window and flexed his arm, one of his tattoos stretching across his bulging bicep. He hollered into the receiver, "When are you going to get sober?"

I took one look at him and collapsed into tears. "Oh my fucking God, what is going on?"

Ric swapped places with Jacob, who took the phone. "David, I'm telling you right now—my whole life has changed. I've had a spiritual awakening. I've been sober for seven months. You can do it too, you know." He told me his story, how during his last week in the hospital, he had rallied and recovered and went on to join a 12-step program. Even though he couldn't keep much food down and often vomited in meetings, he somehow made it through. I couldn't believe my eyes.

As I took in the sight of Jacob back from the dead, a powerful surge of hope flooded through me. After seven months of waiting, with little communication from my attorney about the status of my case, I had resigned myself to being locked up for life. I felt desperate for a miracle, not just for my freedom but simply for an end to all the uncertainty. I didn't want to die, but I couldn't imagine living either, if it meant enduring endless days in this foul and filthy ash heap of human potential. Energized by this unexpected turn of events, I shifted immediately into planning mode. If I had any chance of getting out of this shithole, I needed all hands on deck to galvanize support before the judge.

"Listen, guys, I need your help," I said, my voice cracking with emotion. "I need you to go to everybody you can in all the AA and NA meetings and ask them to write letters to the judge on my case. I'm going to be locked up forever if people don't show the court that I have a support system on the outside, people who care about me. Our job is to convince them that I could build a new life if they just give me a chance." I sobbed into the receiver. "I'm really serious. Promise me, you've got to do this."

"We'll do everything we can, David," Ric said.

At the end of summer 2005, I met my defense attorney, Nina, in court for a plea hearing. She had asked me to be patient while the prosecution built their case. And once they did, she said, "You're going to have to take a plea deal. Federal court has a 93 percent conviction rate. You'll never fight this, and if you do, you're going to prison for a long time." So, I had agreed to plead guilty to possession of an instrument to commit identity theft, and the prosecution agreed to drop the other charges.

Two months later, on September 20, 2005, Judgment Day finally arrived. The transport unit took me to the Phillip Burton Federal Building and US Courthouse in San Francisco where I waited in a holding cell all day long.

About halfway through the afternoon, Nina showed up in the glass conference room adjacent to the holding cell. The defense packet she had put together described my troubled childhood and how I'd been part of the foster care system numerous times. And since I didn't have a long criminal record or a history of being violent or belligerent toward law enforcement, the recommended sentencing was three to ten years. Where I would end up on that spectrum remained a dreaded mystery. My stomach twisted into knots at the thought of even a single month longer in prison.

Within the first few months of being at Santa Rita, I had said to myself, *This is so horrible—I can't imagine spending the rest of my life in a place like this. If there's any chance I can get out, I will never, ever come back*. And I meant it. I often watched someone get released, feeling elation for their good fortune, only to see them return a few days later. "Are you kidding me? You just got out. What the hell happened?" But for some of them, a life of crime and time was the only life they knew. That was not going to be me. That couldn't happen. But I needed a miracle.

"Remember, this could go in any direction," Nina said. "We don't even know what kind of mood the judge is in today. Just don't expect any mercy."

I returned to the holding cell to wait until my case was called. Marius, one of the other inmates in my transport unit, had been confident he would receive a light sentence only to come back from court having received eight years—just short of the maximum guideline of ten years. I asked myself the question that had haunted me for nine months: Would they make an example of me? Or would they give me a chance to set an example instead? I was certain I was doomed.

I hadn't heard from Ric or Jacob since their visit, so I walked into the courtroom uncertain about the outcome of their efforts. Usually in federal court, the prosecutor pleads his or her case and asks for the maximum sentence, and my public defender was then supposed to say something like, "Have mercy on my client because he's really a good guy who got off on a bad leg."

But Judge Hamilton didn't let either the prosecutor, a young white guy in glasses, or my public defender, Nina, talk. "I want to hear from Mr. Wichman," she said.

With sincere remorse and regret, I said, "Your Honor, these past five years, my life has been in turmoil. I'm completely at odds with how I've been living. This isn't who I am."

Judge Hamilton shuffled a stack of papers on her bench. "I have the letters you wrote me, and I have all of the letters from other people written on your behalf. Clearly, they believe in you." Then, she noted, "I'd like to enter into evidence letters from Mr. Wichman's supporters on the outside."

I glanced at Nina, who glared at me. I hadn't stopped writing to the judge, despite Nina's admonition.

Had Ric and Jacob pulled it off? There were people who had known me during the year I'd gotten clean and sober. Had Ric and Jacob convinced them to write and ask for leniency? Was there a shred of hope after all? I found it so hard to believe. No one ever actually writes to the court, do they? Surely no one from the outside would have written in on my behalf—they had their own lives to live. Apparently, I had short-changed the recovery program, as I had so many times over the years. My peers had shown up for me in a way I could have only hoped they would. They wrote in. They represented a world I had longed to be a part of but in which I never included myself. They saw something in me I could never see—they saw hope.

A profound silence settled over the courtroom. Behind me and all around the room, everyone seemed uncomfortable in Judge Hamilton's formidable presence.

"What would happen if I let you out of here today?" she asked. "What would your life be like? Would you change?"

I stood frozen in place. This was my cue to take responsibility for my crime, to apologize to the court and the rest of society, which happens during every sentencing. I knew better than to make excuses or try to make the judge feel sorry for me. This was the one thing I couldn't screw up. If I tried to impress her with any grand plans, she would surely recognize the manipulation. She was no fool, and neither was I.

I looked at the judge and knew I was no match for her. I used to be able to con my way out of any situation—this was not one of those days. I felt a level of defeat unlike anything

I'd ever experienced. I felt a sense of humility and harsh honesty previously unknown to me.

"Your Honor, I don't know what to say," I said, visibly trembling but determined to stand in my truth. "I've never been able to stop using. I've tried everything, but I've never succeeded before. I don't know if I'm going to make it, but what I can tell you is that—" I paused for what seemed like forever. "Your Honor, what I can promise you is that I will do the very best that I can."

My chest sank. My head spun. I was out of words and out of my body. I felt like the loser my stepfather had predicted I would be. Maybe he was right. Maybe I was doomed. I had never been able to stay clean before, so naturally I had very little faith in my own words. I just said them because that was my truth in the moment. I felt my knees begin to buckle. I clenched my jaw, grinding my blackened teeth.

And then the unthinkable happened.

After a flurry of legalese, the likes of which I had never heard before, the judge spoke the words I had waited nine months to hear.

"Mr. Wichman, the federal court sentences you to six months incarceration with credit for time served. You will pay restitution and serve three years federal probation." After the usual legal ramblings for the court record, she looked down at me from her bench. "Something tells me you can do this. There are people out there who care about you. They want you to make it. You need to want to make it, too."

I couldn't believe what I was hearing.

"If I ever see you in my courtroom again," she added sternly, "you won't get out anytime soon. The court will not be so kind to you."

I nodded my head in disbelief. Tears blurred my vision. Holding back sobs, my heart pounding out of my chest, I choked out a barely audible thank-you.

She had a look on her face that I caught just briefly. She knew she had given me a chance. This was my moment—I wouldn't dare let it slip way. I would make it work. After all my prayers, months of deep grief, and a lot of begging to a higher power, I had received my miracle, one that I wouldn't let go to waste.

CHAPTER 14

Once my case had been heard, everything that followed was one glorious blur. Back at the prison complex, I sauntered in as best I could in handcuffs, grinning so hard my face hurt. But I wasn't allowed to talk to anyone or pass notes or do anything on my way to my cell. Even though we regularly violated that rule, this time, I had to contain myself. I wasn't taking any chances.

Throughout my pod, dead silence.

A trustee named Sancho saw me arrive and stopped mopping. "So, what happened?"

I whispered, "They let me go."

"He's getting out!" Sancho screamed.

Laylay hollered from her cell, "WHAT?"

Someone else called out, "Are you fucking kidding me?"

A simultaneous roar erupted across the pod, fists banging on cell doors, deafening shouts of "YEAH! Right on! I can't fucking believe it!" The guards in the control room flickered the lights and told everyone to shut the hell up or no free time that night.

Though it would be a couple of weeks before I was formally released, already the girls were yelling, "Can I get your commissary card? Can I have your socks?"

When recreation time came, our pod exploded into a gleeful party. As happy as I was to be getting out, I felt a sense of sadness to know I'd be leaving this ramshackle family I'd created over the past nine months, people who had been present with me through my detox and my spiritual awakening and improbable moments of joy. Before I left, I took everyone's jail cell numbers. "I promise I'll write you and put a little money on your books."

And I kept that promise. One of the first things I did after I was released was write everyone in my pod a letter, and I included in each envelope a five-dollar money order so that they'd have some cash on their books. In jail, that was a decent amount of money, and it was the most I could do at the time—it amounted to the last sixty dollars I had. To the Christian guys, I wrote, "Jesus loves you. Never lose hope." And I received amazed replies: "I cannot believe you actually sent me a letter and a money order. Nobody ever does that!"

And it was true—nobody ever did. I'd heard endless promises from people I met in jail who swore to me they would find Bob or Richard and send me a letter once they got out. I never received any of their letters, but I didn't hold it against them. I knew it wasn't personal. The world is chaos, especially the world of ex-cons.

On October 5, 2005, federal transport took me to the Hall of Justice at 850 Bryant Street in San Francisco for processing. As I waited to be released, fear struck me, as deep as it ever had, even worse than before my sentencing. Not knowing when I'd be released, I hadn't had much time to plan. Freedom didn't necessarily mean I was going to be okay—I would be homeless again. I had no job, no real place of my own. I had no faith in myself. I was the one who kept falling down and waking up in some alley or flophouse surrounded by filth and used needles. I couldn't resort to the old ways and means of survival anymore.

The county had lost the clothes I was wearing when I was arrested, so I was dressed in some random outfit pieced together from lost and found. I didn't even have a pair of shoes—the shower shoes I'd worn in prison and to my sentencing belonged to the county, so they made me give those up, too. The last gate buzzed, and I placed my bare feet on the asphalt and began walking. The glare of freedom felt foreign and disorienting.

For the next three years, I would be on probation. If I started partying again or committing crimes or acting out in any way, they could lock me back up. I didn't know if I deserved the chance I'd been given, but I vowed to live every single day from that moment onward to make sure I didn't screw it up. All I had was that chance, and I needed to run with it.

Barefoot, I broke into a run all the way to Eddy Street and Leavenworth to the check cashing center run by the Russian couple. I had no money, no place to live. Maybe I could borrow a few bucks from them until my public assistance checks were reinstated. Ric West was the only friend willing to help me out, but he had relapsed, and I was terrified of walking into that space, especially with our long history. I couldn't compromise the terms of my parole—the last thing I wanted was to get shipped back to Santa Rita.

When I arrived, the check cashing center had just closed. It was after five, and the fog had already rolled in, rendering all of downtown cold, damp, and overcast. Without a dollar to my name, I had no idea what to do next. I lingered outside the storefront for a moment, contemplating my limited options.

As far as I knew, Richard was still on the run from the feds. I had no idea how to get a hold of him, but I desperately wanted him to stay free, wherever he was. Just before I was arrested, I'd asked my friend Bobby to take care of Bob. At this point, however, both Richard and Bob's whereabouts were unknown. Every night in prison, I had fallen to my knees to pray the same thing: "Dear God, please let me hold Richard in my arms for one more night, just to tell him I love him. Please let my dog be okay, and let me hold my dog again."

Just then, I heard a tapping on the glass behind me. I turned around to see the Russian—a stout, bearded man with features that looked more Mediterranean than Slavic—waving at me enthusiastically.

"David, come in here! We've been very worried about you." He motioned me toward the front door while he jiggled the deadbolt open. As soon as I walked inside, he said, "We have money for you!"

By some kind of miracle, Richard hadn't taken everything. Another public assistance check had arrived after he cleaned me out. Now I had a little over two hundred dollars in my pocket—all I had to start surviving on my own.

After I left the check cashing center, I stopped in a cell-phone store to buy a new flip phone. In this sort of *Twilight Zone* state of being, I suddenly remembered the phone number for my friend Danny, one of my drugging buddies who used to let me shower and crash at his house from time to time. All the while I'd been in jail, I couldn't remember his number, but somehow it came right back to me. I flipped open my new phone and called him.

"You need to come over here right now," Danny said. "Get into a cab and come to my house."

As soon as I arrived at his place in the Lower Haight, I could hear my beautiful, blond, eighty-five-pound pit bull barking, while Danny repeated, "You wanna see Daddy?" He had Bob! He had my baby!

I dashed up the stairs and flung open his apartment door. My beloved Bob jumped right into my arms. We were both beside ourselves, a crazy, intense reunion. Bob hopped up and down, yelping and crying out. I felt like I was dreaming. Danny, who usually had a hard-core exterior, was a little misty by that point. Bob wouldn't leave my side. A wash of calm came over me, mixed with joy and excitement. I was experiencing yet another miracle. Somehow, whatever forces existed in the universe, my prayers had been heard. I felt overcome by a sense of spirit and a belief in a higher good, some bigger picture.

And this was just the beginning. I found out that Richard had had Bob the entire time, but he often dropped him off at Danny's. Danny said he'd been taking care of Bob, but he didn't know much else. He assumed I knew where Richard was.

Despite the excitement, I knew I had to get out of Danny's house and steer clear of the temptation to get loaded. I took off as fast as possible. The first thing I wanted to do was take Bob to Duboce Park, the exact place I'd seen him last. I walked my precious Bob to the park and took off his leash, and he started bolting around in circles. I joined in, and we ran together in a blur. At one point, Bob was suddenly distracted by the sound of someone approaching. The fog had rolled in, enveloping the park in a dark evening haze. Given my sense of the universe at work, I just knew who it was. Bob ran and leaped into the air onto someone who caught him in his arms and kept walking toward me.

I would know that voice and saunter anywhere—it was Richard.

The moment I recognized him, I made the same mad dash toward him that Bob had and hugged him as hard as I could.

Richard loved Bob with everything he had—he may have been many things, but he was dedicated to our dog. He had managed to stay out of jail and away from the feds the entire time I was gone—a minor miracle in and of itself. His only mission was to protect Bob, which he did.

"Come over and crash at my place tonight," he said. He was staying in a live-work warehouse with many from the same crowd we used to get in trouble with, but I couldn't resist. I stayed the night at the warehouse, and I fell asleep holding him in my arms while he held Bob in his. Basking in pure bliss, I lay there, wide awake, holding my boys. I never wanted to let go—they were all I had.

In the middle of the night, in perfect Richard fashion, he rose quietly—I was crashed out—and left to break into mailboxes with one of his accomplices. Before the night was over, he ended up getting caught.

Just like that, he was gone. I realized I'd prayed to spend *one more night* with Richard so I could hold him in my arms one last time. I was beginning to see how such miracles worked.

The next time I saw him, he was being sentenced to three years in prison.

My attorney, Nina, always said, "David, you need to forget about him. I know people, and he's never going to stop doing what he's doing. You have a chance, so you'd better get your shit together." She was very parental, but she was also right. Richard went to prison, and as far as I know, he's still out there somewhere doing what he always did. Nina, on the other hand, is now representing death row appeals. The woman is a boss.

A few days out of prison, I called Bonnie Schwartz. "There are a lot of programs out there, especially for people just out of incarceration," she said. "You should check out some of the meetings and get connected."

For the next few days, I walked around aimlessly, crashing on Ric's couch at night while he detoxed from his relapse. I walked Bob over to the Castro Country Club, a sober house I'd known about for many years. No sooner had I arrived than the manager, Dan, appeared on the front stoop, holding a broom in his hand. He stood there looking at me. He leaned on his broom, placing his palm gently against his cheek.

In a loving but direct voice, he asked, "Well, honey, are you ready yet?"

His dog, Ricky, ran down the steps to lick Bob—they were both so excited to meet. Dan walked me inside and made me a coffee. I told him what had happened. He just listened. Each time another drunk or addict walked in, he introduced me.

"David needs a meeting," said Dan. "Where are you guys going today?"

Within days of my release, I went to meeting after meeting. One of these guys would drag me to a high-noon meeting or a group that met in some random church basement. This went on for months. I lived off the kindness of these strangers and old friends who were clean and sober. They took me and my dog into the meetings and into their homes. I got connected. This was my new life.

In 12-step programs, you often hear, "I finally got clean when I ran out of my own ideas." Drug treatment programs only work if you're willing to surrender to someone else's way of doing things, and for so many years, that was just not happening for me. But now I was gladly willing to admit that I'd run out of my own ideas. October 8, 2005, became my official sobriety date. Though I hadn't used much while in jail, I drank homemade alcohol, despite the fact that it gave me diarrhea afterward—the horrible stuff wasn't even worth it.

My first sponsor after prison was a guy named Mikey, a handsome gay guy and a hard-core AA Big Book thumper with the kind of dogmatic zeal exhibited by religious fundamentalists. He rode a supercharged motorcycle and preached about being helpful to others. Mikey took me to men-only meetings conducted according to strict black-and-white approaches to recovery.

"If you've come here to get better," he said, "then you're here for the wrong reason. This program isn't about you. It's not about you getting sober. You're sober right now, and that's all that matters. If you've been clean for two weeks, that's more than the guy who just walked through the door with no hope at all. This program is about you helping that guy. Yes, you! That's your only job right now. If you do a few simple things, you might get better in spite of your best thinking, which is what got you here to begin with. If you stay, you might have a chance."

I liked his approach, and I needed it. That kind of abrasiveness helped me survive—it's what worked to get me clean in the beginning. I was still confused, broken, shattered. I believed with all my heart that I needed fixing, and the only fix I'd ever known was a drink or a syringe full of speed. For once, I had direction. I fixated on recovery. As I continued to get clean and sober, my life transformed rapidly. My perspective on the fundamentalism of Alcoholics Anonymous has evolved since then, but in the first year of recovery, the structure and rigidity and my sponsor's no-nonsense approach saved my life.

When I eventually started sponsoring guys new to the program, I became a fundamentalist Big Book thumper myself:

"You look like you're ready to get loaded. Go help somebody!" There was nothing gentle or airy-fairy about my approach. "Do you want to live, or die? You don't do it my way, you'll die." The people who used the way I had couldn't hear niceties. We were just off the battlefield, deaf from the chaos. The wake-up call could easily be lost in the gentle voices of those who cared just a little too much. The desperation of a drowning man was necessary to get clean long enough to see the purpose of living this new life.

After my release from Santa Rita, I had no job or any way of supporting myself, so I took Bob and a couple of dogs who belonged to friends in AA and went to various dog parks. Dog walking had become a booming industry in San Francisco, and being an ever-resourceful survivor, I devised a plan to become a professional dog walker. Dog walking felt like second nature—dogs have always gravitated toward me, and I bond and connect with just about any canine I come across. In the park, I struck up conversations with other dog walkers. "Yeah, I just started out in this area a couple of months ago," I lied. I had no choice. I couldn't dare let on that I wasn't a real professional, though I can't imagine many of them were either.

Every day, I scoured the internet for instructional videos on dog behavior and training. I watched endless episodes of *The Dog Whisperer.* Almost none of it mattered; every dog was so different. I had to learn by doing—jump in, make mistakes, try again. I got the hang of it pretty quickly. Eventually, the dog walkers who needed to refer out work or felt they couldn't take a dog in an area they didn't service began to pass along new dogs to me.

I also hung flyers all over town, and I printed up cheap business cards that said "David's Daily Dog Walks" along with my cell-phone number. I made friends with people in the program who had dogs—usually former drug addicts and alcoholics who had taken their dogs through hell and back, just like I had with Bob. I walked a few of their dogs for free to start my pack and further convince other dog walkers around town that I was legitimate and could handle my pack.

When I first started out, I walked dogs for half the price of what most walkers charged, simply because I needed the business and didn't know what I was doing. I placed a low value on my time because I had zero self-esteem, and most days I felt like I was just winging it. But more and more people took a chance on me, a career criminal and dope fiend from the street. Many of these dog owners knew my story and by some cosmic turn entrusted me with their most prized love. Humbled and determined, I began to grow my new career.

My ex Ric West, who has since gotten clean himself, lent me money to buy a used Mazda B2000 pickup truck with a camper shell, and soon I was driving my sober posse—a riff-raff pack of one-eyed, three-legged, scalawag dogs—to Fort Funston on the southwestern edge of San Francisco, a decommissioned military defense post situated on bluffs two hundred feet above the Pacific Ocean. Trails lead down to the shoreline and to the only area in Golden Gate National Parks where dogs are allowed to run off-leash.

When I backed my truck into a spot in the main parking lot and opened the tailgate, a half dozen dogs came flying out onto the field. The steep, mile-long hike through the woods down to the beach took about an hour because I had to play with the dogs, maintain control of them, and stop occasionally to pick up poop. The minute we hit the shore, they all ran for their lives to the beach. I carried a little sack of treats on my belt at all times, so if I wanted to get their attention, I whistled, and they knew to come to me for a treat. Other dog walkers came over to strike up a conversation. Everyone was convinced I had total control of my pack. The truth was that it was a dance I had to learn quickly or else those dogs would have owned me. I played catch with the dogs, and they ran around the sand or leapt into oncoming ocean waves. Bob often swam far into the water and dragged back huge vines of kelp across the beach.

I felt intensely connected to this pack, and they became my spiritual committee. Throughout our days at Fort Funston, I contemplated how I was going to work through my problem *du jour* or play out the rest of my life, a meditative state where I often came up with answers as I tossed a ball or ran alongside the dogs. In early sobriety, I endured a lot of growing pains in letting go of old ideas and learning how to live. A plethora of changes happen early in sobriety after years of living in insanity. Suddenly, you're asked to be an adult and be responsible and pay bills or parking tickets—things I never did while in my addiction.

When you're new to recovery after living a life of despair for so long, even paying the electric bill feels like a spiritual experience. My first utility bill came from Pacific Gas and Electric. As I held the envelope, looking at my name through the cellophane window, my heart began to pound. The fear from all the unpaid bills from decades past mounted inside. Would they ask for all the money I owed up to now? I thought about whether I would have to apply for a bill-forgiveness program or argue with someone to keep the lights on—I was so used to trying to game the system that it had become second nature. I had been so accustomed to thwarting my responsibilities; I had grown so ready to fight.

I took a deep, frustrated breath. *Just get on with it!* I ripped open the envelope. The bill amounted to a grand total of $14.32. *That's it? Ha! Well, I can pay this. No problem.*

Walking over to the Green Apple Market on Polk Street to buy a money order was the first stage of an entire experience. I inserted the money order into an envelope and addressed the envelope to PG&E and affixed the stamp—all in a surreal, slow-motion state of awareness. An unnameable feeling overcame me, and tears began streaming down my face. An upwelling of sadness, then gratitude, then excitement. As odd as it may seem, this was an awakening, one of many defining moments that marked my restoration. I was being responsible and accountable. I felt the swell of some sense of self-esteem, and then I understood. I got it. My spirit begged me to see this moment for what it was. If I had a guardian angel, she was probably breathing a huge sigh of relief. "Finally, he did it!"

I had spent decades getting loaded because I couldn't stand being who I was. I would do anything to not live in my body, and every penny that ever crossed my hands went to ensure I stayed loaded. Money wasn't money; it was access to dope. It never lasted because it all went to drug dealers. Not just money but everything I had of any value. If I could trade it or sell it, I used it for drugs, for oblivion. But now, in this moment, I felt just a little more like a human being. I watched people meander across the road as if I were watching a movie on a screen, only this time I was part of the story.

Living by the spiritual principles of accountability and integrity were greater than simply paying a utility bill. For thirty years, I hadn't done anything normal. By the end, I had resorted to writing checks in other people's names, defrauding banks, and stealing from stores. The delusion of addiction is that a life of crime and despair is the norm and that it's okay. I truly believed that I was doing what I had to do in order to survive. The drug addiction seemed justified. Having that illusion smashed—seeing that living that way is fucked up and harmful to everyone—is a rude and harsh awakening. It's easy to feel like a total piece of garbage for living that way, and it's no wonder many addicts never get clean. They stay immersed in the shame of what they did while in their disease. I could walk a bit more upright among others. I began to feel a part of the world we live in—just through this simple act of paying an electric bill.

This pack of random dogs, but especially my own beloved Bob, bore witness to these changes. Within seven months, I had a full pack of sixteen dogs, which I split into two groups and walked on different days, Monday through Thursday, from eight in the morning until three in the afternoon. The dogs started out crazy, chaotic, and unruly, but within the first few years, we settled into a rhythm. They helped me develop a reliable pattern to my day—this is what we do, this is where we go, and then back into the truck to go home. They helped me create the most stability I'd had in my life in decades, if ever.

In early October 2007, a photographer from the *San Francisco Chronicle* happened to be at Fort Funston. After asking me a few questions about my dog-walking business, he asked if he could snap a few shots for a feature story the newspaper planned to run about the $40 billion a year pet industry.

"Just go about your day like you normally would," he said. "I'll be the creepy guy following you with a camera. Pretend I'm not here."

He was a nice guy who probably took to my pack because we were joyful and enthusiastic. We had a lot of energy. Or maybe I was simply in the right place at the right time. The photographer followed us around, snapping a few action shots as I tossed a ball to my dogs from a red ball launcher. Pocket, one of the pit bulls in my pack, attached himself to the photographer. Pocket loved people, especially those who paid attention to him. He was a ham, so the scene was set.

When the article came out on October 9, I was picking up a golden retriever named Luna from her owner's house in Glen Park. One of the neighbors was outside waiting for me to arrive. "Are you David?" she called out. "Look here! You're in the paper!"

"What do you mean I'm in the paper?"

She held up the day's *Chronicle*, and there was the beautiful action shot of me playing fetch with my pack, plastered across the front page, along with my business name and phone number. The photographer had asked me a few questions about my dogs, but I had no idea what to say. I totally lied—I said I had a website called DavidsDailyDogWalks.com, which didn't exist. As soon as I saw the article, I made a mad dash to buy the URL and to enlist the help of a tech-savvy friend because, even though I was skilled in computer crimes, I couldn't write code. I had no clue how to build a website.

Eventually, people saw my picture and business name, and I added more dogs to my pack. I ended up being one of the more successful dog walkers in San Francisco. For someone who hadn't had a whole lot of successes, the publicity was spectacular, a golden ticket. I felt like I had finally arrived.

CHAPTER 15

When I first started out as a dog walker in the fall of 2005, I made very little profit, barely enough for gas. I had it easier when I lived at the halfway house, where I received public assistance, food stamps, and other help from city programs, but after I moved to my own apartment in the Tenderloin, I still struggled to pay the rent. I also needed to pay for gas, treats, insurance, and other costs associated with my dog-walking business. My recovery was flourishing, and I enjoyed being a fully functioning member of society for once, but the cost of living was becoming almost impossible—I needed an edge.

So, I did what I knew how to do. I started escorting again, meeting with clients an hour at a time. I discovered a website called Rentboy where I could post a profile and upload photos. Websites like Rentboy and Daddy's Reviews, where clients reported the good or bad news about the guys they hired, made the work much easier and safer than it used to be—escorts had a means to chat with one another about client issues, and clients could discuss the effectiveness and trustworthiness of the escorts. It was a whole new ballgame, far away from the dangers of the street hustle.

I loved being an escort—it was new and exciting, and the money was fantastic. Along the way, however, doubt and uncertainty crept in. I sometimes questioned the legality of my work. And the internet never forgets. Would this follow me for the rest of my life? What about safety? Sometimes I wondered if I should be escorting at all. Sex work, and sex during recovery, carried a stigma in the 12-step community. Gay men associated sex with drugs—I found it hard to talk about casual sex without someone thrusting into the conversation a warning about impending doom. But then I met someone who would change my mind about escorting for good.

I received a call from a man who lived only a few blocks away, so I figured I would walk over and see him, make a couple hundred bucks, and be done with it. When I arrived, he buzzed me into his building, and I climbed a few flights of stairs to his apartment. When the door swung open, a disheveled older man dressed in sweats showed me into his front entryway. Halfway down the long hallway into his home, I noticed a bunch of needles on top of a dresser. *Ugh, this guy is a druggie—I can't be here.* For a second, I considered leaving, but then I decided to just get it over with and never come back again.

As I walked into his bedroom, he sat down on the edge of the mattress. He had a broad chest and a strong, slightly overweight body, and he looked impossibly tired. I could tell he was suffering. He seemed almost afraid of me. *This is never going to work.* He dropped his sweatpants to the floor and began fiddling with something that looked like a latch or a strap on his left leg. I watched as he removed a prosthetic leg fitted just above his knee. He looked up at me again, his left leg in his hand, and asked, "Is this going to be okay for you?"

Given his defiant tone, I knew he was fully prepared for rejection. But whether from pride or compassion or some mixture of the two, I hopped onto his lap, looked him in the eyes, and said seductively, "We're going to have the time of our lives."

The fear on his face dissolved. I watched relief wash over him as he realized his amputated leg wouldn't affect my willingness or ability to provide for him this service. Our intimate interaction wrapped up rather quickly, as it didn't take him long to finish. Something beautiful had taken place between us. I felt like I was there on purpose—squarely placed in a room where I had been left with no choice but to be open and intimate and to fill the room with acceptance of someone who clearly needed it. A rush of energy and conviction flooded my being.

On my way out, I took a closer look at the needles on the dresser. They were a different size than ones used by IV drug users—I realized they were for insulin. He had diabetes, which evidently had cost him his leg. During our interaction, I noticed his other leg was dying from poor circulation as well. Had I left right away, assuming he was a drug addict, he would have felt rejected for his illness and disability.

Emerging from his building into the cacophony of Geary Street, I sat down on a curb and flipped open my cell phone to check in with my then-boyfriend, Kurt, a calm, gentle, and sexy man I'd met online when I was about fifteen months sober. Our lovely relationship had become my safe harbor and jumping-off point. Kurt loved me and believed in me. He saw things in me I couldn't see in myself, and he gave me the courage I needed to feel good about the work I was doing. He meditated daily, and he taught me a lot about gratitude and staying present. He also taught me how to give and receive with no expectations.

When we first met, I refused to smile. My teeth were in such bad shape that I had practiced long and hard how to hide the decaying bottom set. I brushed and rinsed constantly, and I was never without a breath mint. One day, Kurt caught me at the mirror. He had noticed my shame long before he figured out what was happening.

"Let's do something about this," he said. "You're so handsome—you need to have these fixed."

He was instrumental in having my teeth reconstructed, a long and expensive process that completely changed my life. He called the best dentists in the city and made the first of many, many appointments. My first session lasted almost eight hours, but when the dentist finished putting the temporaries in place, all evidence of my meth addiction had disappeared. For the first time in years, I smiled a full smile, one I could be proud of. For once, I saw myself as truly desirable.

Kurt's gift will last forever. He and I are very close to this day. I still call him in the midst of my experiences—when things are tough and especially when something incredible is taking place. He knows the power and joy he has brought to my life.

Back then, we established a practice for my security where I would call him after an escort session to check in. I was glad the appointment with the diabetic hadn't taken long because a flood of emotions had threatened to overtake me. Waiting on Kurt to answer, I broke into tears. He heard me crying as soon as he picked up the phone.

"You okay? What happened?" he asked.

"I don't know what's happening to me right now," I said, "but this is what I'm supposed to be doing. I just know it."

"Of course it is. I've been trying to tell you this for a long time now." He was always the comforting voice on the other end of the line.

Though I didn't understand it at the time, the universe was steering me toward a higher calling. The dog-walking business had provided the profound grounding I needed, but I sensed it was time to grow and move on. I knew it was a huge risk. I was so confused. I believed in the often-repeated adage, "If you do what you love, you'll never work a day in your life." I was already doing what I loved—waking up every morning and running with my dogs on the beach. They were my life. I was already in my element, living the good news of love and connection. Escorting was a curveball I hadn't counted on.

I had a really great life, and yet I felt pulled, drawn, even called to escort work full time. By 2008, I had become wildly popular as a sex worker. I had my own website, and I created amateur sex videos that were passionate and unique. My channel attracted more than 14 million viewers. I had, without reserve, made the choice already—the internet would never forget. Emails poured in, and bloggers wrote about this unassuming escort who did things a bit differently. During my first year in the world of online sex workers, Daddy's Reviews named me Escort of the Year. I started getting calls from out of state. I flew to places like Manhattan, Dallas, and Oklahoma City for overnights. It wouldn't be long before I started traveling overseas to places such as Paris, Jamaica, even China.

I knew it was time to shift course. I had hired one of the guys I sponsored in AA to fill in for me when I needed someone to walk my pack, but I soon realized I had to make a choice. Though my heart was filled up by those dogs, I was being pulled in a different direction. I finally made the decision. With a heavy heart, I gave my clients three months' notice and began the process of matching other dog walkers to my precious ragtag gang of dogs. I knew many amazing dog walkers—that was the easy part. What was toughest was saying goodbye. I believed in what I was doing; I just didn't know if it was the right choice. Obviously, an undercurrent within society says sex work is bad. Choosing this work, no matter how much I believed in it, always left me with doubts and old, leftover ideas.

On the final day of David's Daily Dog Walks, I picked up the few dogs I had left for one last walk to the beach. Saturday was usually my day off, but I chose that day so I could say goodbye to the families who had given me not just the keys to their homes but to their hearts. Most of my dogs had been rescued from shelters, so I was well aware of their keen sense of change. My heart pounded with longing and fear. I felt like I was letting them down. For years, I had been the pack leader—strong, confident, stern, and in charge. I was crazy in love with each of them. They counted on me for that daily trek to the beach, and I counted on them for so much more. We were connected on such a deep level that I couldn't fathom our time was ending.

I finished the beach run that day and walked the dogs back to the truck. I opened the tailgate and did my usual call out, "Up!" and up they went, one by one, into the truck, eagerly looking to me for one final treat before the gate closed. I stood there frozen in time, gazing at these innocent, beautiful beings.

As the dogs wagged their tails, a calmness came over me. The tailgate was still open. I felt a strong desire to crawl into the back with them. *Say a proper goodbye, dummy.* I lay down in the bed of the truck, staring up at Pocket and Bob, who were already lying by my side, poking their noses in my face. One rested his head on my shoulder and the other on my lap. We just lay there. Then, I curled my body around the two little dogs, Benny and Emmi Lou. I began to sob uncontrollably. Walter, the ever-loving Spanish water dog, clearly baffled by my outburst, licked my face with vigor. I sat up and hugged him. I sat there in a daze. They all just stared out the back of the smelly truck with me. I said goodbye to each of them, kissing and hugging them. To any passerby, we would have looked ridiculous. But I could feel everything being settled.

As I made my way to the cab, I realized I had never climbed into the back of the truck except to make adjustments and clean up. I had never been just part of the pack; I was always in control. Making their safety and joy my job, I was always top dog. Today, I was just another puppy in the pack, and they knew it. It had always been easy to understand what was happening in their rapidly beating hearts. Dogs are transparent. You just have to look closely. They speak to us, and we understand them. Dogs love without question, without measure. When you're in their pack, you're in. Dogs are teachers; they are messengers; they are gifts to understanding love. This pack taught me to love, no matter what I'm doing. Now it was my turn to go out and embody this same truth and share this lesson with the world.

I closed the tailgate and drove off into the late afternoon fog. I dropped my pack off for the last time. David's Daily Dog Walks had come to an end. For once in my life, I hadn't been fired or tossed out. I hadn't run away or thrown in the towel. I closed up shop with grace and integrity. It was 100 percent uncomfortable and hurt like hell, but nobody said living by these principles would be easy.

During the years of my addiction, I'd unwittingly garnered a wealth of training being in situations with people I'd never imagined I would encounter. Now that I was sober, I found myself approaching these same people from a new perspective, one full of compassion and acceptance. The guy who had lost a leg to diabetes was only one of many clients who had been disfigured by illness or accidents and carried enormous loads of shame about their bodies.

In March 2009, I met Mark, a fifty-something retired schoolteacher who lived in Washington, DC. I was working a circuit where I would spend a week in DC, a week in New York, and a week in Chicago, meeting clients who responded to my ads. When Mark emailed me, he said, "I don't want to hire you for sex—I just want you to come over and spend some time talking. I just want some company." He went on to write in great detail about his situation.

I knew what he needed, and it wasn't conversation. I knew he wanted love and intimacy, and he needed it to feel organic. The money always ruins the fantasy for guys like Mark, at least at first. At this point in my escort career, I loved my work and knew I was helping people, but I had certain boundaries to keep me from getting overly involved. My clients and I were going to get close, but I still had walls up. Sometimes, I tried not to get too close, especially if I wasn't going to see them again or develop an ongoing relationship. I felt there had to be a barrier, and oddly enough, that barrier was sex. If a client didn't want to have sex, I was reluctant to book the appointment. Sex was my protection, my guarantee that the encounter was all business. I barely knew myself, so letting clients in wasn't easy and took years.

"That's not how this works," I wrote back. "I'm happy to meet up and have a conversation, but we will be getting it on."

On the day of our appointment, Mark called to cancel. He felt self-conscious about his body, and yet he was so lonely, he insisted that he just wanted some company. "I really can't go through with this," he said. "It's not who I am."

"Look, I need you to trust me on this," I responded. "When I walk through the door, let me take over, and you relax. Can you trust me, Mark, just for a moment?"

He agreed, and we hung up.

When I arrived at his tiny studio apartment in Dupont Circle, Mark greeted me at the door, leaning on a cane, an orange tabby cat curled around his legs. As soon as I crossed the threshold, he lit a cigarette and began repeating the details from his email about his injuries, his ex, how he could barely afford to hire me.

He'd had ten operations in nine years, including intestinal surgery after a bout of cancer. He'd had two strokes. After the last one, he spent two months in a coma and woke up to find his right side paralyzed. His partner of many years left him at that point, taking everything. He was still rebuilding his life, or what was left of it, in a shitty apartment with just a cat for company. He walked with a cane and a severe limp, and he was very self-conscious about his scars and his wilted leg.

I could tell how intensely needy Mark was—he hated everyone but desperately needed intimacy. I wanted to silence his steady stream of negativity. We passed stacks of paper and clutter until we reached his living room and settled onto the couch. I tried to unbutton his shirt, but he resisted.

"Can't I keep the shirt on?" he begged.

I stopped what I was doing, taking in the terrified look on his face. "Listen, let's be quiet for a moment." I reached out and caressed his cheek, looking deeply into his eyes. "Would you mind if I kissed you?"

He consented, so I kissed him softly and began gently unbuttoning his shirt. When I peeled off his shirt and saw the thick, rigid scar, I understood why he felt so ashamed of his body. I ran my hand along a giant S carved into his skin across half his mid-quadrant, unlike any scar I'd ever seen. He looked like he had been ripped apart and sewn back together.

"Everything about you is perfect and beautiful," I whispered.

His wound mesmerized me, the way it felt, the way it affected him. Somehow, I believed that bringing Mark's awareness to his scar would help him see what I saw—something interesting and unique. I sensed intuitively that the deepest roots of his shame were also his gifts and his message. He was called to serve the world through his experience of pain. With his depth of courage, he had a lot to offer, but he needed to heal himself first.

So many of us hide our shame and inability to accept ourselves. Many people gain weight to protect themselves from intimacy and getting hurt, often without realizing they're doing so. Everyone puts up walls, and each person expresses it differently. People suffer from the stigmas and isolation around disability or sexual fetishes involving gender, age, weight, race, whatever it might be. When someone hired me, and I recognized they were ashamed or insecure, I made it a priority to shine a light on it. I had to be completely unaffected by it, which was a delicate balancing act. Total acceptance granted them immense relief and eased the pressure I felt in figuring out how to best serve them. Oftentimes when a person is truly seen and accepted, they lower their walls a bit, leaving just enough room to build some trust. This gives everyone in the room permission to accept themselves and move toward healing.

I started to remove the rest of Mark's clothes. He resisted at first, shaking and whispering, "No."

"You agreed you would trust me," I said.

When I began kissing him deeply, I could feel him let go. He completely relaxed. I could tell he hadn't been kissed this passionately in a very long time, if ever. I had to help him position his lips and jaw and coach him to move his tongue with more ease and affection, rather than push through it to get things over with. His fear and resistance subsided in exchange for intense, hungry passion. I sensed how important it was to caress the very parts of him he considered a source of shame—I moved my mouth down his body, kissing the traces along his scarred hip, his thin and withered leg.

As a provider, I have to suspend the idea that there's anything unacceptable about someone. I have encountered people in various states of depression and isolation, many of whom have foregone nail-trimming and certain levels of hygiene required for sexual intercourse. In Mark's case, as he surrendered to the pleasure, I cast out all such concerns. I combed my fingers through his hair, flaking off the dry skin from his scalp. I spent forty-five minutes just loving him, from his stringy dark hair to the scaly skin on his back. He hated all of these things about himself, but my job was to show him he could love himself back to health.

I took his stiff fingers, one at a time, and stretched them out, caressing his palm. He vacillated between a state of resistance and full surrender, most of the time not wanting such intimate touch because he didn't understand it, but he soon realized how desperately he needed it. We moved deeper into a rhythm of beautiful, passionate love-making and aggressive deep kissing. We weren't just fucking but something much more intimate, powerful, and healing. At the end, we both experienced a deep, intentional orgasm—pure magic.

I left his home feeling good about our appointment. The funny thing is that Mark never hired me again, but he did write one of the most meaningful reviews I've received over the years. These reviews from appreciative clients didn't always chronicle my sexual acts but highlighted the healing properties of what we do when we care for our sexual health and well-being.

Mark wrote, "David is a healer, and I thank God for him coming into my life. He looked at me and made love to me. I have never had a man make love to me as David did. I still get teary-eyed even thinking about it. David is wonderful with an intuition for what someone needs. I hope to meet him again. If you have suffered and don't know your way back, David is a God-giving guy."

The guy who had lost his leg to diabetes had brought home the importance of what I was doing, but there was something about my encounter with Mark that proved to be a turning point in my career. I felt to the depths of my being that this was healing work.

Mark stayed in touch by sending me emails from time to time. He went on to recover fully and marry a guy he met while out for a walk around his neighborhood, and the two of them moved away to a small town in New England. I followed him on Facebook for a number of years. About five years after our encounter, Mark passed away from pneumonia. His death tore his husband apart. What struck me was how changed Mark was by the end—a once lonely man who died loved and terribly missed. He was one of many men I met who carried deep, embedded shame about how horrific and unattractive they believed their bodies to be. But he became an activist in his small town, outspoken and courageous. Though his courage had been there all along, he had buried it beneath his self-loathing. Hiring a sex worker helped him start that journey to excavating his hidden treasures.

Not all of my clients have been struck down by severe illness or emotionally paralyzed by deep sexual shame. I have been with men from all walks of life, many of whom know how to take care of their needs and are adamant about living full and healthy lives, which includes great sex.

When you're gay, bisexual, or sexually fluid—anything outside of society's idea of normal—you're afflicted with shame right out of the gate. Families, teachers, classmates, communities, and, of course, religion have taught countless generations of LGBTQ men and women that they were born broken, inadequate, and inferior. As opposed to guilt for wrongdoing, shame is wrong *being*. Suicide, depression, and self-loathing are all markers of a shame-based belief system. If a person's sense of self is steeped in wrongness, they don't feel they belong. They feel separate and abandoned. Countless children experience this isolation every day. They grow up and carry that sense of separateness into their thirties, forties, even into their seventies. Sometimes clients have come to me to be relieved of that shame, even if just for an hour.

Men immersed in shame and loneliness isolate themselves from the world. But they still want to be touched, kissed—and yes, even fucked—so if they can bring a sex worker into their life, it's a huge win. I have watched men emerge from the depths of despair and go on to find life partners, change careers, move to places they never thought possible, all because they found the courage to love themselves. They cracked open the shield that kept them trapped in the lie that said they were somehow undesirable or unworthy of great love and, yes, great sex.

I believe that intimacy is a necessary component of the human experience; we each need physical and sexual connection to another human in order to feel we're part of something. We need it like we need food, water, and exercise. If you get sick, you see a doctor. If you get hungry, you eat. The body needs touch like the lungs need air. It's amazing what we give up because we think we're not acceptable. When people go years and years without touch or sexual relief or the acknowledgement of their presence, they can get sick in mind, body, and spirit. The evidence of this truth surrounds us every day. A culture of violence, hatred, and alienation permeates the planet—the direct results of a lack of love and intimacy.

Many people have bought into the illusion that they are unworthy of love or don't need it. My work has reminded me that we are all worthy of intimacy and connection with another human being. I am only a conduit of healing—I'm there to push away whatever might be blocking the truth. Sex work has taught me more about toxic shame than most sex therapists can even imagine. All around the world, I see evidence of an epidemic of loneliness and despair. My work is just my small contribution to bringing a measure of intimacy to another human being. So many people have bought and paid for the idea that they are broken. These men come into my space closed down, buttoned up, frozen in their shame, guilt, remorse, and self-hatred. I feel compelled to clear that sexual shame so they feel less alone.

Somewhere out there is a four-hundred-pound man with scaly psoriasis all over his body, who hates himself and feels miserable and horrified to be naked. What I'm called to do is jump in and accept him right where he is in the moment. That is the miracle of sex work. When I'm truly present and all of his fears fall away, I know I have delivered a message of acceptance, matched only by my passionate embrace. My actions say, "I'm all in. I'm here for you, and you can trust me." He lets go and lets me in, and then I know that this work matters.

I too grew up in shame and self-loathing. I believed the voices throughout my childhood that told me I was ugly and unacceptable. Even when I was trying to hustle on the streets, I felt I had no value because I lacked the popular look, that Adonis body. As a skinny and unattractive new escort, I figured I'd accept the clients who would accept me. What I discovered was that not everyone was looking for perfection. They were looking for a connection, and in so many ways, so was I. I know without a doubt that my work has healed me more than I could ever heal anyone else. As I have found the beauty in others, I have seen my own beauty a little more clearly. As I have helped others realize their own truths about loving themselves and accepting themselves right where they are, I have found myself loving my truths and loving all of the things I once thought were so wrong with me. These experiences were as healing to me as they were to the men who hired me.

One of my earliest clients, a man in his seventies whose lover had died forty years earlier, once said, "You have no idea how good you are at what you do. You give so much for so little."

I was like, "Yeah, right. Sure."

He took my face in his hands and looked me straight in the eyes. "Listen, you really are unlike anyone else I've ever seen, and I've hired them all. There's nobody like you right now. I want you to raise your rates—you're selling yourself short."

That same client wrote my first review on Daddy's Reviews. His words helped me realize that I had been given a gift, and I needed to embrace it and respect it. At the time, my self-esteem was pretty low. A long time would pass before I realized the importance of this gift that enabled me to see beyond the surface and uncover where I was most needed—and that it mattered.

As my clients started talking among themselves on the internet, I continued to grow in popularity, and my client roster expanded rapidly. At 12-step meetings, I shared how spiritual my escort experiences were, describing my awakenings. Some people shamed sex workers and porn actors who were doing it by choice and feeling good about it. Many of them feigned acceptance, delivering clichés like, "Keep coming back," or "This too shall pass." Others just said, "It's wrong, and you're going to get loaded again."

I stuck to my convictions. I believed in myself. I found many supportive friends both in and out of the recovery community. These people and many of my clients became my tribe and chosen family.

I'm reminded of my experience with Norman, the pedophile who molested me when I was six—it was all just a game until he told me I was going to hell. As soon as a person has been shamed, their behavior becomes dark; they feel they have to hide it and keep it a secret. When someone in recovery bottles up shame inside themselves—especially unfounded accusations pronounced by others—that shame can lead to a relapse, giving the naysayers a chance to say, "I told you so."

I pushed back against such assumptions in those meetings by being very vocal about my work. Meanwhile, I stayed sober year after year and successfully sponsored many sex workers. I would tell them, "What you're doing is absolutely okay. Have your experience. If there's a problem, we'll figure it out. If it's not for you, we'll move away from it."

Escort, sex worker, prostitute, whore—call it what you will, but I love what I do. The puritanical moralists demonize sex work and natural human needs. Laws have long been in place that harm sex workers and create an environment that punishes people for having consensual sexual encounters. The archaic system of shame-based legal hoopla has kept sex workers dodging systems that have been in place to control and enslave them for centuries. But selling time is not selling sex. That is how escorts provide their services within the confines of the law. If there's a connection between two adults, and they choose to engage in sex during the time they're together, then it's still selling time.

Navigating and defending sex work is an exhausting, upward trudge. Many providers and allies find themselves overwhelmed by increasingly stringent laws and regulations that limit their ability to provide safe and effective care for their clients. One such regulation is FOSTA-SESTA, which stands for the House bill called the Fight Online Sex Trafficking Act and the Senate's version, the Stop Enabling Sex Traffickers Act. FOSTA-SESTA has turned out to be an intensely overreaching law that has failed at its original intent, driving true criminals farther underground and out of the reach of law enforcement. The law has inflicted adult website providers, online advertisers, and banking institutions with policies that are now stricter than ever, placing many marginalized sex workers at greater risk and forcing them to return to the conditions of street prostitution.

Even though sex work can be primal, it's about a lot more than sex. As a sex worker, I don't just walk into a room, take off my clothes, and start fucking. I see the emptiness or fullness of the moment. I look for a need and fill in that space. I take on what might be missing or add to what is already there. What makes for a successful male escort is someone who makes his clients feel important, like he really cares and wants to be there—because he *does* want to be there.

Sex work isn't just the world's oldest profession; it's a rich and sacred tradition that dates back throughout human history. Most of the escorts I have encountered have been wise, resourceful, and useful members of society—people who pay their taxes and serve their communities and raise money for AIDS and other causes. They not only offer healing to the lonely, the rejected, and the dying, they also provide a space for people to explore their secret kinky desires without shame.

CHAPTER 16

As my name and reputation in the world of male escorts rose in popularity, my time became much more valuable, and my life once again took off in a new direction.

One of my most important clients was a man name Liam, who turned eighty-six in 2019. I first met Liam when I was still living at the halfway house. His wife had died the year before, and at age seventy-five, he was newly out of the closet. A native San Franciscan, Liam had been brought up a devout Catholic. His brother had come out a few years before, divorced his wife, and married another man. That gave Liam permission to explore his long-repressed sexuality once his own wife passed away.

During our earliest encounters, we met at the Hot Tub and Private Saunas on Van Ness, a spa built in the 1970s. Each private room boasted a hot tub, redwood sauna, shower, and massage table. After an hour at the spa, we ate tacos at a taqueria on Polk Street. We saw each other about once a week, always the same routine. We often carried on deep conversations lying on the bed in the spa, and soon, Liam and I had become very close.

I wanted to help facilitate Liam's coming out, so I began introducing him to other friends in the gay community, and I convinced him to go to dance clubs and circuit parties and festivals like Folsom Street Fair—rites of passage for young gay men but unheard of for guys who spent their formative years still in the closet.

One day in 2009, Liam said, "I'm thinking about going to Africa, and I want you to consider coming with me."

My dream as a child had been to run away and travel the world—I would escape late at night into the garage to look through my stepfather's *National Geographic* magazines. I spread out maps to find places I planned to see when I grew up. I lost that dream for decades, my only international adventure—the ill-fated backpack trip through Mexico—ending in complete ruin.

"You name a price, and I'll go," I said.

"Well, it's a long trip, seventeen days. What would you want me to give you?"

"First of all, I don't even know how I'd price that. But I want to go so badly, I'd go for free."

"Absolutely not. This is a business."

I blurted out a random number I thought I could live with, certainly more than I'd ever made in a month but way below market rate for travel escorts.

"That's ridiculous," he said. "This is a seventeen-day trip."

He wrote me a check for the market rate and even gave me a tip at the end of the trip. The deal was done. Liam recognized my value much better than I did. The amount was a gold mine for me at the time, and I would finally get to go on a safari!

Liam and I traveled to East Africa to the Serengeti National Park in northern Tanzania. We joined a tour group of fifteen people staying in luxury tents on the plains. One afternoon, as we peered from the top of our army green Land Rover, a short way across the plain stood a black rhinoceros, a critically endangered species that's been decimated by poaching.

I held my breath, my camera posed just in front of my face. Liam stood behind me on a ladder, both of us in silence. Just as the black rhino emerged from the bush, a little baby came up behind her. The two of them had leathery, charcoal-colored hides, but neither of the baby's two snout horns had yet developed.

Several other Jeeps pulled up in our vicinity. A woman began to cry quietly, moved by this beautiful moment. A heavy silence hung over us all, punctuated only by the occasional clicking of cameras. We watched the mama and her calf meander the plain, chewing vegetation. We were experiencing a precious and incredibly privileged moment—one of only twenty black rhinos left in Tanzania, and she'd given birth to a baby. Our guide told us the baby, named Blackjack, was the twenty-first. (As of 2019, the population has risen to 167, thanks to the import of rhinos from South Africa.)

Back at camp that night, everyone was high as a kite, awed voices asking, "Oh my God, did you see that?" We sat around a campfire all evening, talking, bonding, sharing our memories of the day. As I looked around our circle at these faces glowing from joy and the heat of the flames, I realized that if Liam had traveled alone, he wouldn't have anyone at home to reflect back to him the magic we had witnessed. We wouldn't have anyone to call ten years later to reminisce about that time we saw one of the few black rhinos still in existence.

Tanzania was my first destination with Liam, but we also went on several gay cruises to Italy, Spain, Croatia, and Cuba, and we traveled to France and to New Zealand, where we went bungee jumping off of a cliff in Queenstown. We got along great, and we learned a lot from each other. Liam has always been there for me. Few clients have grown as close to me as he has. Without a doubt, my professional success has been a direct result of his encouragement. More importantly, Liam has taught me so much about being true to my word and true to myself. He gave me permission to shine and be proud of the provider I had become.

When word got around that I was going on high-end travel-companion trips, my value went up significantly. Many considered me out of reach and too busy—a reputation I didn't want. I still loved seeing my hourly clients, but high-end travel and extended adventures was a dream come true. There exists a population of gay men—older, successful, retired, widowed, or otherwise alone—who long to share unique experiences with someone else, which is a big part of traveling. An adventure is so much more memorable when a person can reflect back on the experience with someone who cares about the trip as much as they do. Sex is part of the package, but the experience is so much more than that. This demographic was wealthier or had saved more resources for a once-in-a-lifetime trip. I brought energy and enthusiasm to every adventure, and we always looked forward to hot, fun, passionate evenings.

That's how the Male Adventure, my adventure travel business, got its start. Soon, I found myself on planes, trains, and ships at sea, being wined and dined around the world. In the decade since I founded the Male Adventure, I've traveled to every continent, including a month in Antarctica, visiting countless countries across the globe.

Not all of my clients aimed for adventure when they traveled. When I first met Gregory, he preferred to relax in a lounge chair at the Four Seasons in Punta Mita, Mexico, sipping margaritas. He was a high-powered business executive who valued his downtime. I, on the other hand, had a low threshold for lounging around. Spending four lazy days at that resort near Puerto Vallarta made me want to jump out of my skin.

One afternoon, lounging near the shore, I turned to him and said, "I just want to make something abundantly clear to you—we're not a match."

"What do you mean, we're not a match?"

"I love adventure travel. I'm happy to see you for an hour or an overnight in New York City"—I'd seen him many times that way—"but taking vacations where I just lie on the beach is the most uncomfortable, awkward feeling ever."

"What do you want to do?"

"I want to go scuba diving or bungee jumping or see wildlife."

We started talking about our options, and the next time he contacted me, he asked, "Would you be interested in going to Indonesia?"

"Sure, but we need to plan that trip and make sure we're busy actually doing things," I said.

In the middle of our trip to Bali, I suggested we get certified to scuba dive. Our first attempt at certification was a disaster—the dive master, who didn't speak English, tried to teach us in a shipping lane. I decided I hated scuba diving and had no intention of doing it again, until sometime later when I took a trip to Maui with another client. We had paired up with an escort friend of mine and his lover, and they were all divers.

Though I was content to simply snorkel, my friend set me up with a patient diving instructor who convinced me to try breathing through a regulator in a swimming pool, and before I knew it, he'd led me to a stretch of shallow water along the beach. Underwater, I saw a bicycle and a lounge chair with an umbrella shading a skeleton—sculptures of sorts placed there for beginning divers. A green sea turtle entered the scene, swimming peacefully, and I was immediately enamored. I returned to Maui a few weeks later to finish my certification.

Gregory followed my lead, doing pool dives in New York City. It took him a long time to get the courage to relax in the water, but once the scuba diving bug took hold, our list of places to visit lengthened by leaps and bounds. He could no longer imagine lying around in a lounge chair, drinking a margarita.

Each time I embark on a new adventure, I find myself in the midst of a spiritual awakening, a delight in the dynamic world we share, not just with each other but with all living things. I do my best not to take any of it for granted. I don't always realize it in the moment, but I can get ungrateful. The ever-present forgetter switches into gear, triggered by the little things: the hotel is a shithole, the driver is a jerk, the towel is stiff and rough, the food sucks. Then something will happen to bring me back to reality.

Since our initial trip to Bali, I've returned to Indonesia on numerous occasions. In December 2015, Gregory and I took this giant trip that cost tens of thousands of dollars to sail on the Alila Purnama during its first season on the water. The handcrafted Alila Purnama looks like a nineteenth-century pirate ship but with the interior of a luxury hotel. We embarked at Sorong and sailed to Raja Ampat, an archipelago in the West Papua province of Indonesia. Raja Ampat is a celebrated marine sanctuary where divers travel to see the extremely rare wobbegong shark, a harmless creature that looks like a shag rug. Sometimes it takes traveling to the farthest corner of Indonesia and thirty different dives to encounter this one rare shark.

The people marketing the Alila Purnama gave us the impression that this would be the most amazing dive of our lives, and we might as well give up scuba diving afterward because we'd never be able to top it. Needless to say, we had high expectations. But once we were on the ship, we discovered that the captain was an arrogant asshole, a complete egomaniac. He demonstrated all the signs of an inexperienced dive master. For reasons I still can't explain, he had no idea where the dive spots were—he kept dropping us in horrible places. On one dive, I looked back at Gregory as he crawled across the sea floor until he got caught in a bed of fire coral. We had been dropped in a current raging out of control. Gregory spent the rest of the day on land, receiving steroid injections to quell the inflammation.

The entire weeklong trip turned into a nightmare. Just before every dive, I asked myself, *What's going to happen now?* Despite my disappointment, the trip turned out to be a spiritual lesson in humility and letting go.

At one point, I went to the captain to express my frustration. I felt personally responsible for my client's experience and wanted this trip to blow his mind. I take my clients to sometimes grueling destinations, convincing them they need an adventure, and if things fall apart, they may not book any future trips. I was afraid, and I wanted these last couple of days to improve, so I enlisted the captain to make sure that happened.

I was careful to be as kind as possible, but given his over-inflated ego, he was clearly disturbed—he thought the entire trip had been a huge success. Astonished by my well-spoken but highly critical feedback, the captain was just about to answer when the crew came running from the kitchen and pointed over the deck railing into the water. They were shouting in their native language, and when I looked to the captain for a translation, he said, "They see a shark."

I peeked out a doorway over the side of the ship and knew right away that was no shark—it was a manta ray. I yelled out to everyone, "Mantas! Let's go!" We threw on our fins, masks, and snorkels and slid gently into the water. For about an hour, two mantas swam around us, doing their dance. We could feel slight stings from the tiny jellyfish the manta rays were feeding on, but the discomfort was worth it.

The captain joined our group in the water. We were finally witnessing something incredible, and while the experience was still marred by a long list of things that had gone wrong, I knew I needed to get grateful and get grateful fast. Resentment is like poison—it infects everyone inhabiting the same space. Gregory was certainly happy I had gone to bat for us, but I wasn't helping anything by remaining in a steady stream of internal and external resistance to our situation.

On one of our last dives, we were diving after dark beneath a dock where there was supposed to be cuttlefish and octopus and possibly a whale shark, but we found nothing. Just rocks and white sand. I felt consumed by irritation and annoyance. I was pissed off all over again. The captain was once again my target, and I was once again the victim. I was fuming mad that he had chosen a dive site that was basically a dead zone. *This dive isn't good enough. My business will suffer! He has put our lives at risk.* The chatter in my head became so loud and insurmountable that I just wanted it to stop. I screamed as loud as I could, letting out a thunderous blow of air through my regulator. In the distance, I saw the lights of other divers searching the seabed for hidden treasures of nudibranchs and tiny crustaceans. None of it interested me.

Out of the corner of my mask, I saw a stray blue blur, a weird-looking fish that I now know is called a scribbled filefish, a creature with a tubelike mouth and scales that look like

a child finger-painted it in uneven dashes of neon blue. It's such a common fish with thousands of different varieties that no one cares about them or bothers to take any pictures. He floated upright—his tail toward the surface of the water and his head aiming down at the sand. This was how they slept, I supposed. I sat still, gazing at him. He floated toward me, his fins spinning behind his gills. His colors grew brighter and more intense the closer he came. Exhausted from my inner war, I just surrendered. I realized this was it—this fish was the most beautiful thing around. We floated together in the stillness of the water. My breathing slowed, and the rhythm of my heartbeat tuned into the energy and awareness of this silly experience.

That's when it hit me.

It wasn't the captain who needed to change the sea or my circumstances. It was my job to change my perspective of the journey and dig myself out of the hole of negativity. I'm the one who needed to find the gift in each moment. My thoughts went from pondering this beautiful, common fish to observing the sand that glowed in the pale shafts of moonlight coming through the water. I remembered a line from the Sufi poet Rumi: "You are not a drop in the ocean. You are the entire ocean in a drop." I looked across the sea floor, focusing deeply on every grain of sand. I imagined that each grain of sand contained the possibility of hope. In the vast deserted darkness of this reef was a single, beautiful fish, shining brightly, surrounded by an infinite wealth of possibility.

My consciousness had shifted enough for me to finally get over myself. I was overwhelmed with gratitude, along with a bit of stern and righteous remorse. I chuckled. *You're a fucking idiot, David. You've got it made. You could be in an alley somewhere with a needle in your arm, dying of AIDS. Dying! But you're alive. You're here.* The voice of my sponsor rang out in my head. *Your only job is to be grateful and help others. This is not about you.* I knew I had lost my way, and as always, the universe had its funny way of telling me to get my act together. I was reminded that, no matter what happens, I always have something to be grateful for. No matter how horrifying things might look on the surface, or how delayed the flight is, or how much the lost luggage cost, it's all a gift. Every bit of it is gravy.

The endless sandy sea floor settled out of view. The filefish glimmered across the dive site and swam off. As other divers headed toward me, I finally got it. I had to step back and let the sea and the moon and the stars be what they were, their beauty unobstructed by my own inner clutter. By bringing compassion and gratitude to what was happening right in front of me, right where I was, I could trust that things would work themselves out.

More than twenty years after that first LSD trip, I was accessing higher consciousness without the acid. I may never have known to seek out this awareness if that first acid trip hadn't taken me on a journey of deep compassion. The path to forgiveness is compassion and understanding. We don't always have to forgive, but we grow when we have compassion. Back then, I was awakened and given a glimpse of the truth. I see that as a gift. But I don't need a drug to experience the wonder and oneness of existence. The connection comes from within.

told them I preferred triad to the more popular term "thruple." To me, a thruple is a committed three-way relationship. I went on to state clearly that I didn't dare have such expectations, and I couldn't imagine being in an exclusive relationship with one person, much less two other people.

Besides, I was a sex worker, a message I was sure to send home to them. As far as I was concerned, it takes a special kind of person to date a sex worker, someone confident and sure of himself and completely okay with being open. I was deeply involved with my clients. My only rule for anyone I dated was that they had to accept the whole package, which meant my work had to be factored in and not an issue.

After I returned to San Francisco, we talked over the phone about what it would look like if we dated. Todd was clearly captivated by me, and Carl was delighted that Todd was so excited to have a new man in his life. Nothing was lacking in their world. As a matter of fact, they made room for more love, and they'd had an agreement all these years: "If something or someone makes you happy, then I am happy for you. I am happy with you. I want nothing more than to see you happy."

We took another gay cruise together, and I returned to Palm Springs a few more times. I had clearly fallen head over heels in love with Todd the first night I met him, though I was afraid to admit it. Carl, on the other hand, was a hard nut to crack. He was welcoming but a bit closed off. He was also such a loving man, jumping full bore into this crazy idea of a triad. I fell deeply in love with Carl as well. How could I not love the man who loved Todd so much? They were both cut from the same cloth—honest, loving, kind, and generous beyond measure. We all have our quirks and shortcomings, but I had a hard time finding any in these boys. We had very few arguments. We accepted each other right where we were.

In April 2012, Carl and Todd flew to San Francisco and packed up me and my beloved dog, Bob, who was about twelve years old at the time. We bought a home and invested in a couple of businesses, while I continued to do my work. We spent the next few years in a beautiful, sexy, wonderful, connected relationship.

Carl's courage and determination to explore this new world meant he was often left feeling a bit on the outside. Todd and I encouraged him but also gave him space. There was no need to force it. However, I could tell he was resistant. He's a one-on-one type of person, but he joined in and made the best of it, until 2018 when he fell in love with Caesar, a man he met on a charity bike ride down the coast of California, who is now his husband. The four of us still live together in our beautiful home, no longer sharing a bed. We are two couples, yet we are a family.

After Bob and I moved to Palm Springs, Todd and Carl showered us both with a love we could never have expected. My beloved blond pit bull had been my constant companion, my only son.

From early in my drug-addicted days, Bob witnessed my darkest despair, and in my recovery, he witnessed every challenge and every victory. After I closed down David's Daily Dog Walks, I spent almost all of my spare time taking him to the dog beach in San Diego, buying him steak dinners at Black Angus, and treating him like the royalty that he was. His uncle Ric West cared for him when I went on long trips around the world.

I dragged him from 12-step meeting to 12-step meeting, and Bob made an impact on almost every person he encountered. As I recovered from life in hell to a life of dreams, Bob healed with me. I credit my beautiful Bob with every lesson I learned, every pit of sadness I managed to escape, and every success I achieved. There was no other dog like him. Whether I was roaming the streets, homeless and strung out, or sneaking him into hotels all over the Bay Area, Bob gave me a reason to live when I thought I didn't have one anymore. He was a gift from the universe.

He was there through it all, my lifeline so many times and for so many years. My gentle giant felt the breadth and weight of a life fully lived. I owed him more than I owed anyone. I felt responsible for the pain and suffering and uncertainty he had endured in his early life, and I spent the rest of his life making good on the promise I'd prayed in prison to be reunited with him and hold him again. I had spent many days and years in recovery, singing to him, telling him how much I loved him, and holding him every night we were together.

By 2014, Bob had grown old and weak, and he couldn't get around like he used to. On February 9, Carl called me into the living room. When I walked in, I saw him and Todd standing over Bob. We looked at each other in silence. We all knew we might be at the end. I gently picked up Bob and carried him to the car.

We drove to the vet's office, a few miles away, only to find it closed. After a few knocks on the glass door, a vet tech came out and let us in. The interior was so quiet. A sense of reverence descended on us all as we waited. Bob was exhausted. He just lay there, his breathing slow and labored.

Once the veterinarian entered the treatment room, I asked her to be honest. "I don't want Bob to be in any pain," I said, "nor do I want him to feel, even for a second, that my arms aren't wrapped around him."

The vet didn't even attempt to skirt the truth, which I appreciated. "It's time," she said.

For months, I had been preparing myself for this moment. I was a mature adult. I said things like, "When the time comes, I will be okay with it. We had fourteen wonderful years together. I mean, when he is done, I will be happy to let him go." I joked, "Who wants an old dog who is suffering?" I couldn't stand the thought of falling apart or making a big deal of his death. After all, we had lived through a lot together. I rationalized and minimized the reality because I didn't want to face the truth.

The vet gently inserted a needle into Bob's vein, and he quietly passed away in my arms. Not a single flinch, just peace and relief.

I was *not* expecting what hit me next.

The most gut-wrenching wail exploded from the depths of my broken soul. The pain was so deep that I just lay there on the floor holding my baby and screaming, "No! No! No! God, please help me! Fuck! Oh my fucking God, this hurts! This is so painful!" I went into a panic. Then I whispered, "Please, God, make it stop! No, no, no, nooooooo! This is so fucking painful!"

The boys stood by, just holding me and caressing me. I think they were a bit shocked to witness such a meltdown, but being the truly beautiful humans that they are, they stood by and let me fall completely apart.

I was catatonic as the boys guided me outside to the car and drove me home. For the next few days, I fell into intermittent

upwellings of the most beautiful, gorgeous, and yet horrendous, painful feelings of grief I had ever known.

Though I hadn't been prepared, somehow these painful outbursts also brought welcome moments of remembrance and love, a love so deep that it shook me. I spent day after day combing through videos and pictures of my life with this dog. He was such an important part of me. Losing him felt somehow beautiful and courageous but also so ugly and unfair. My love for him was so deep and ingrained that I felt his loss in every cell of my body. I had no idea our bond was so profound until it was gone.

I always knew that Bob loved me without question and without measure, and in the end, I was absolutely certain he knew how much I loved him, even when I couldn't love myself.

CHAPTER 18

The Male Adventure, which Liam serendipitously inspired me to launch, also led me to the loves of my life. My travel work has become a vehicle for pure joy. I'm not a mere observer of life anymore, looking on with empathy or sadness or a need to give or receive; I'm the embodiment of gratitude on every trip. I take on the role of cheerleader. I try to see the positive in all of the complexities of an adventure. I pass that energy onto those I travel with, which is an incredible feeling.

Creating the Male Adventure was the manifestation of a childhood vision—my dreams were coming true right before my eyes. Deep down, I always knew I would see the world. I knew my education would come not from books at a university but from villages and the citizens of the planet. I knew my back would always be carrying a pack on it. I used to think I would travel the world on my own because I didn't belong anywhere. I thought I didn't fit in. It's true. I don't belong anywhere because I fit in everywhere.

I never guessed that I would dive in the waters of every continent, hit runway shows in Milan, paraglide over South Africa, or trek through the Ugandan mountains to gaze at the Silverback gorilla. I never imagined that I would swim with humpback whales whose mating songs reverberated through the ocean and deep into my soul—yet that was the seed I had planted long ago.

As an escort, I thought I was making money to pay the rent, a means to an end, a pseudo-shortcut to earning an income because I didn't have the education or skills to make a living any other way. What happened, despite my best thinking, was this incredible journey of growth that has landed me in one spiritual awakening after another, having encounters with the source of life in everything I've seen. Even among my greatest and most profound ideas, never did I imagine a life like this. For so many years, I lived out an utter nightmare, but now I'm living my dreams.

On many of these journeys, I've had profound, life-changing interactions with wildlife—endangered East Timor deer on Moyo Island in Indonesia, Silverback gorillas in the mountains of Uganda, rescued elephants in Thailand, and street dogs in Cuba. Even wild dolphins at sea, who used to avoid humans, have taken to interacting with divers for belly scratches. Their eyes pierce my soul; they see right into me.

One experience I will never forget happened shortly after I was certified to dive. Carl, Todd, and I went to Puerto Vallarta, Mexico, and hired a boat to take us scuba diving. As we descended into the deep blue water, a juvenile whale shark the size of a fishing boat began circling us, my first encounter with this majestic species. At first, I assumed he was enjoying our bubbles because he kept swimming above and below us. After the whale shark circled me a few more times, I noticed the real reason. A few meters away, a giant black manta ray was struggling. I shot off like a bullet toward the manta to see what the problem was, and as I came closer, I could see the ropes of an old fishing net cutting into her cephalic lobes back to the wingspan. I grabbed the remaining net attached to the rope to try and lift it over her giant wing. Although she was

still able to swim, the net dug deep into her flesh, and I feared I would only make the situation worse.

I alerted the dive master, and he bolted toward the manta. He was carrying only a dull blade. The stress was palpable. We struggled to keep up with this twenty-foot behemoth, swimming around her, our hearts pounding, determined to set her free. At last, the dive master made one last cut, and the rope to the net broke free. The manta swam off into the unknown.

We conducted a safety stop and emerged alongside the dive boat. Just then, I heard Todd yell, "David, look down!"

I peered into the water below to see the whale shark surfacing—he was swimming directly toward me. He swam into my arms and into my belly, moving his head up and down. If Todd hadn't captured everything on video, I wouldn't believe this story at all. The whale shark seemed to be thanking me. As silly and impossible as it sounds, this juvenile whale shark who hunts with mantas and feeds on the same diet wanted me to know we helped. I climbed back onto the boat consumed by elation and intense joy and began crying out loud.

I didn't sleep well for almost three days afterward. I knew these creatures had delivered a message, and to this day, I know exactly what they communicated: We are their only hope. We must take care of the land, the sea, and the air, and we must stop the poaching and environmental devastation taking place across the planet. As crazy as it sounds, I've looked into the eye of a mother humpback whale and heard her in my spirit as if she were asking me to speak up. I can no longer remain blind to what I know is true—the planet is begging us to be better caretakers. With these encounters comes a responsibility to share the joy and be good messengers.

In 2017, I traveled to Isla Mujeres, which might have been a questionable destination given my relapse there all those years ago, but I had become quite secure in my spiritual condition. For several years, I had been immersing myself in spiritual teachings from the New Thought movement, a metaphysical worldview that our inherent nature is divine, our thoughts create our reality, and we have access to Infinite Intelligence, as well as "A Course in Miracles," which seeks to remove all conscious blocks to the experience of Love as the only true reality. In returning to Isla Mujeres, I was coming full circle and face-to-face with a reflection of my former self.

As I walked along the beach one afternoon, I found myself in the same place I'd relapsed in 1998. The beachfront palapa was no longer there—the spot now a series of new condos and hotels. I thought about the pain I'd been feeling that day I drank a margarita—how desperately I needed to fill a deep void. The crux of my addiction in action was an attempt to run from pain caused by believing in this sense of brokenness. Something else happened on that trip to Quintana Roo that made me realize how much inner work I still had left to do.

That afternoon, our group embarked on another dive trip, this time to see Cancún's Underwater Museum of Art, called MUSA. I had seen pictures of this place on the *National Geographic* website, a series of five hundred life-size sculptures by English sculptor Jason deCaires Taylor, each affixed to the sea floor and crafted to encourage coral growth, a living interaction with the ocean. I had long wanted to experience this incredible underwater site.

I swam past a Volkswagen Beetle and a group of businessmen crouched next to their briefcases with their heads buried in the sand. In other sections, vast groups of people dressed in traditional Mexican skirts and cowboy hats were tied together with what looked like rope or cable, all of them symbolically connected to one another.

When I swam through the middle of this group, I saw a little boy sitting on an upside-down paint bucket, head bowed, hands clasped between his knees, face covered in a thick coat of vibrant red algae. All of the other sculptures had their backs to him, and none of their rope included him.

This underwater image just destroyed me.

As I swam to see other sculptures, I found him again and again in various spots around MUSA. Though the little boy haunted me, I didn't dare look away. I looked into the eyes of this same child, over and over again. I went from one sculpture to another, rediscovering his facial expression and body language beneath different stages of coral growth. But no amount of coral or algae could hide what I saw: a childhood poisoned by fear, shame, and disappointment. I saw myself the day my parents picked me up from my grandmother's house and told me they had a surprise waiting at home. I recognized the terror and defeat in that six-year-old's face.

Behind my scuba mask, my face felt hot as I remembered all over again the shame of being forced to throw my soiled sheets, pajamas, and underwear in the washer while my stepfather spanked me, one crack for each piece of clothing. No one could feel me. No one could see me. Nothing my stepfather did to me in the years afterward broke me as completely as he did in that incident in the garage.

A rage of frustration emerged. *When will it end? When will I finally just get over it?* This childhood trauma no longer

defined me. I had done the work! I lapsed into unforgiving self-talk. *Why can't I grow up? When will enough be enough? You're such a victim—twelve years sober, you should be over this by now.* The undercurrent of unresolved pain is brutal and insidious. These are the unseen scars of a scapegoated child. I wondered whether I would ever heal. I was just like, *Fuck! Why can't I just move on?* My emotional state vacillated between injured and caretaker, trying to nurture my own soul.

Before I swam away, I prayed a short prayer and said goodbye to this little ocean-encrusted David sitting alone and despondent. An overwhelming sadness came over me. Seeing myself in the MUSA sculpture proved to be a significant turning point, not just for me but for that little boy inside who never got the love he needed.

In late March 2018, I joined my life coach, T. J. Woodward, and clinical psychologist Adriana Popescu at a Conscious Recovery weekend workshop at the Ralston White Retreat in Mill Valley, California. T. J., an author and spiritual teacher, had been my life coach for the year before the retreat. He had taught me a new approach to addiction recovery, one that recognized that underneath all self-destructive behaviors is a whole, perfect, beloved Essential Self. My spiritual path had been a long journey toward remembering who I truly am, inseparable from all of life and Love itself.

I stayed with twenty other attendees, many of them early in sobriety, in a huge, three-story mansion near the woods at the base of Mount Tamalpais. During one of our sessions, T. J. and Adriana led us through an exercise on the inner child. In 2015, around the time I'd had ten years of sobriety, Shari

sent me a photo of four of us as kids—Shari, my stepsiblings Lurlene and Trevor, and me—all of us in pajamas, posing with a doughnut the size of a salad plate, my tiny fingers digging into the edge of it. I noticed in my six-year-old face dark depressions around my eyes, as if I'd been crying or upset before the shot was taken.

When I first received this photo, all of the dark memories from that era came flooding back: Norman's molestation, my stepfather's abuse, my mother's surrender to her husband's will, the hope I harbored all those years that one day I'd get the love I longed for from my parents. I often hoped that one day my parents would stand before me with open arms and say they were sorry, that I didn't deserve what had happened, and that they should have protected me. I dreamed of witnessing their remorse and receiving their love, maybe even an apology: "We never meant to hurt you." But it was never available to me. Even in my twenties and thirties, I had returned again and again to a dry well—the love I needed was never there.

Shortly before the retreat, Donnie sent me a different picture, one of just Donnie, Shari, and me. I was even younger in this photo, before any of the abuse had started—a happy, chubby-cheeked baby with big eyes and a huge smile, leaning forward with laughter. Unharmed and invincible, the only thing this child knew was love.

At the retreat, the facilitators had us take out our cell phones and bring up a digital image of ourselves from childhood. If we didn't have a baby picture on hand, T. J. gave us time to call someone and ask them to text us one. I pulled out the pictures Donnie and Shari had sent—I saw them as Innocent David and Broken David. As I looked at the fat, happy, laughing version of myself at three years old, I couldn't

help thinking how that child lasted a year at best before this abused, broken child took his place.

"I want you to look at your picture and recognize the innocence of that child," T. J. said. "You're talking to the innocent, unbroken child, letting them know you're taking care of them and taking them on a journey. Everything that happens in life from here on out, they're with you in that state of innocence, reminding you of who you really are."

The exercise fell flat—it just didn't resonate. Inner-child work seemed so cliché. I mean, how 1985 of them to do this! *I'm not going to waste my time.* But then my thinking shifted. *Just be here. You have nothing to lose.* My judgment was no match for what was about to take place.

Meanwhile, the session continued: "I want you to picture yourself lying in an area of safety, whether that's a backyard or at a beach, and just be with your child in a safe setting."

I imagined sitting on a grassy lawn with Broken David, stringing daisies together. The facilitators guided us through a visual meditation on caring for the child, connecting with him, being present, and just seeing what came up. After a few minutes, I heard one of them say, "Now, tell the child they're safe. Begin returning to the room, and when you're ready, you can open your eyes."

For whatever reason, perhaps because of my inner protector, I didn't just say, "You'll be safe" to my inner child; I pictured unrolling an orange mesh fence around him several times. I got really into creating a dramatic visual. I said goodbye, reassuring him that I'd be back. Then, I returned my awareness back to the room.

As I looked at those two pictures on my phone, the only thing I couldn't wrap my head around—and to this day, it's the struggle of my life—was how in the world a grown adult

could raise his fist or remove his belt or wield the heel of a boot and try to destroy this child. Not just once or twice, but for years and years.

There was a theory by Dr. John Bradshaw in the 1970s and '80s about large dysfunctional families in which one child bears the weight of all the punishments, and everyone can point their finger and say he's the one. I became that scapegoat in my family. Everything wrong became, "David must have done it." Many times, I probably did do it. But the worst part was my mother's abusive shaming, while she stood on the sidelines, allowing whatever was happening to happen, because she had no ability to recognize me as a child worthy of love and care and kindness.

To even admit this fucks my head up. It just destroys me. It's the one hurdle I can't get past. As much as I want to believe that my soul came here to learn a certain lesson, to forgive the unforgivable, to align myself with the higher consciousness of love and compassion and empathy for others, no matter what, this is the roadblock. You just don't do that to children. You just don't. You can't.

I've found it easier to heal from childhood sexual assault than from my parents' abuse. It's the hardest pill to swallow—the hardest part of the work to heal—and I fear I might never get past it. I could have been lighting schools on fire, but no matter how badly children might behave, you don't withhold love, treat them like animals, lock them up, beat them, humiliate them. How does such a person live with himself? If I'd ever done something like that to a child this young and vulnerable and innocent, I wouldn't be able to forgive myself. I would spend the rest of my life apologizing and feeling completely horrified by my actions. I wonder too about the other adults, the aunts and uncles

and bystanders. It would destroy me as a human to witness something like what was happening.

Therapists often say to their clients, "They were doing the best they could with the information they had." Oh no, they weren't. My parents refused to acknowledge that their behavior was cruel and damaging. Instead, they painted an entirely different picture of what occurred in my childhood: "Are you kidding me?" my mother once exclaimed. "None of that happened. We protected you." Shari was the only person who ever validated my experience, defending me in the midst of the abuse, and suffering from it herself for the rest of her life.

That's why the inner-child exercise was so tough for me. I fell apart; I was dying inside. Broken David had been the persona who had shown up many times in my past to remind me of how useless and hopeless and worthless I felt. I realized I had never taken care of him or nurtured the wound created by all the trauma. Broken David hated himself. He believed to his core that he was unworthy of any sort of love. I reflected on Pocket, one of the pit bulls in my pack when I was a dog walker. Fearful and traumatized, he had been abused in a fighting ring. He acted out almost daily. He needed a lot of attention and love. The pack never cast him out; they always attempted to nurture him. Broken David was wild, almost feral, but he was here and very present. I felt called to show up and accept him, right where he was. Maybe he was ready to heal. Maybe I was ready to face him.

As I looked at that photo, Broken David became an entity, a living being who needed help and could be healed through love, acceptance, and encouragement. My thoughts flowed freely. *No matter what happens from here on out, I saw everything you went through, and I'm here for you now. What happened was wrong, and I'm here to protect you.*

As we shared our experiences with the circle, I dissolved into a flood of tears. I had never taken the time to love this little child. I had never realized how his requests for love had gone unanswered. There was no reason for his caretakers to brutalize him. Little David never had any of that coming.

After the ninety-minute session came to a close, I was exhausted.

"Everyone needs to go do something by themselves for a while," T. J. said. "Relax, take a nap, go for a walk, or get some food, and just be with this experience."

I instinctively perceived Broken David, the child in the picture, standing next to me. I couldn't visually see him, but I could feel him. He was smaller than I imagined him to be. I walked out to the front porch and stuck out my right hand. I imagined him wrapping his tiny hand around my finger, and then I gingerly walked him down the stairs to the woods.

I kept looking at him, sharing in a silent communication. I gave him a chance to walk and be distracted and to sort of look around as if he were coming outside for the first time in a really long time. I walked onto a trail that had a creek running through it. I looked down at this little child and perceived him with this mischievous smile. He took off running, and I took off running, and we started splashing through the creek together. We ran and ran until we arrived at a trail head.

As we strolled along, I struck up a conversation out loud. "We've been through a lot together. It's been so hard. So painful and isolating. I was very lonely and sad. I'm so sorry."

Anyone walking by would have thought I was the strangest person in the world. Intuitively, I knew I was convincing *myself*, but I needed to go through this. I needed to acknowledge him and pay attention to him. He had needed me for more than forty years, and I had stashed him away until he forced

his presence on me with angry, negative self-talk, an inner voice that said, "You're not good enough." I imagined him rocking back and forth, repeating the traumatic words said to him by those who were supposed to love him. "Liar! When will you grow up, David! This shit has to stop. Look at you! I can't stand the sight of you!" Over and over again. It broke me to visualize it.

I shook my head to snap out of the memory. "I don't want to live that way anymore," I blurted out, pointing my walking stick in the air as if making an oath. "And by the way, I don't want to be broken anymore. And I don't want you to be broken anymore either. So, here's the deal. No more Broken David. I want you to be Amazing David. Incredible David. Magical David." I called out like a fourteen-year-old playing army in the woods, the echo of my words permeating the trees. Tears rolled down my face, and my voice started cracking. "And from now on, I'm going to do my best. I'm here to protect you, and I swear to you, I'll never let any of that stuff happen to us again. We're in this together. I'm going to love you. I'm the love you've been waiting for. I'm the love *we've* been waiting for."

I set down the walking stick I'd been carrying and lowered myself onto a small wooden bridge that crossed the creek. I curled up in a ball and cried my eyes out. I needed to purge this pain, not just for my own healing but for the inner David who needed me. When my sobs quieted, I looked up at the sun as I talked to Broken David, who was now Amazing and Magical David, and I could perceive him releasing the grip on that giant doughnut, his tiny face a little less afraid. As we sat there, I clearly perceived him whispering, "Okay, I hear you."

Through the blur of tears, I saw a tiny white butterfly land on the tip of the walking stick. As I admired this creature,

a symbol of transformation and soul evolution, the butterfly fluttered in a circle before my face, going higher and higher until I couldn't see it anymore.

I sat up and silently took David by the finger again and pulled him over my shoulder and onto my back, and then I walked, as if I were carrying a forty-pound child, back to the retreat in total peace. I couldn't believe I had waited forty-nine years to do this. Even after enduring so much horrible pain and confusion, I can say now that Broken David has been a gift. He gave me this story. Remembering the sculpture at MUSA, the inner-child process at the retreat helped me remove the fire-colored algae from that little boy's face. I brought in my own cable, my own connections to him. "You'll never be alone," I assured him. "You'll never again be in the midst of a large community with everyone's back to you. You will be in the middle of it, helping hold everyone together."

This brokenness that proved to be an illusion had been a huge part of my identity for decades. Part of me had been proud to stand on the mountaintop crying out, "Hey, look at me, I survived! You motherfuckers will never get me again!" From a spiritual perspective, the only thing broken and proud of its survival was my ego. It is still very much a dance.

Entire swaths of life are predicated on the idea that we have problems to solve. Religious indoctrinations declare that we have all fallen short of the glory of God. For more than sixty-five years, 12-step recovery has commanded addicts and alcoholics to admit their powerlessness in order to receive wholeness. We automatically believe that there is a problem, and we are programmed to try to fix it. What if everything is exactly the way it is so that we have the agency to choose what and how we deal with what's in front of us?

What if certain events happened in order to teach us to love better, to have healthy boundaries, to guide us toward our souls' work?

When I consider the life I live now compared to twenty years ago, I'm overcome with a deep sense of awakening and gratitude. I try to approach my recovery not from a place of brokenness but of wholeness. Wholeness doesn't mean I don't encounter loneliness or anger or any of the everyday emotions of the human experience. I profess no Zen Buddhist ability here. But I don't have to say I am a drunk, or I am a drug addict, or I am a thief, a cheat, and a liar. I don't have to repeat the prophetic gospel of "Once an addict, always an addict." I can hang something different on my "I am" statement. I can choose words of integrity and generosity and wholeness of spirit: I am sober. I am present. I am here. Better yet, with a laugh, I can say, I am Amazing David.

The "I am" statements in a 12-step meeting are meant to keep us humble, but they don't change our humility. They never truly embody a remembrance of our healing. They just mark where we came from. If we are living one day at a time, then today is an amazing day indeed. The fact that we have lived to tell the story is the miracle. There is nothing arrogant about gratitude.

I have done numerous workshops and practices since that retreat at Ralston. Today, after some deep breathing, I sometimes include mantras to cue me into a state of relaxation. I'll begin by saying, "I am the sun and the moon. I am the sea. I am every grain of sand. I am all that there is: the pain, the change, the chaos. I am the darkness and the light. The scum of the earth and the water to wash it away." I breathe some more into the silence, and when thoughts interrupt, I return to the breathing. I meditate this way to unlock the remembering

of who I truly am—one with all that is and a messenger of this wholeness.

The poet Rumi writes, "Your task is not to seek for love, but merely to seek and find all the barriers within yourself that you have built against it."

I would add, "And then share it."

CHAPTER 19

When I was a baby, my parents had me christened in the Catholic Church, a usual rite of passage even for people who didn't practice their religion regularly. Shari, only a toddler herself at the time and already my fierce protector, didn't care for this ritual. As the priest held me over the baptismal font, sprinkling water on my small, round scalp, she yelled out, "Stop it, you stupid asshole! Don't do that to my brother!"

When I was in elementary school, during recess, I liked to perform a dead-man's swing from the monkey bars in the boxed-in tanbark. Bobby Schaffer, the biggest kid in our class, liked to knock me around. One afternoon, before he could throw the first punch, Shari flew at him in a rage and pushed him backward. "Don't you *ever* pick on my little brother!"

The bullies at school knew that picking on me meant they would answer to her. From the earliest age, she had an intuitive protection mechanism—watching out for me was her job, her place in our world. The fact that she couldn't protect me from our stepfather haunted her for the rest of her life. She internalized every blow inflicted upon me; my trauma became her trauma.

She had the first of her three sons, Craig, while she was still in high school. Two more sons, Jacob and Justin, came along a couple of years later. For years, she suffered from the

most severe level of major depressive disorder, a manifestation of the deepest despair and isolation I could imagine. Poor and fighting to stay afloat, Shari often joked that if it weren't for bad luck, we would have no luck at all. Among all the small-town lingo she picked up while in Missouri, that one saying rang truer than true. She lost a husband to suicide, and soon after, her disability and Medicaid benefits were cut off. She was homeless for more than nine months with no way to support herself. She was floundering.

When she finally mustered the courage to contact me, there wasn't much I could do. I can only imagine the kinds of environments she found herself in as a result of not wanting to be a bother to anyone. Over the years, I had done everything I could to help her. I sent her money for food. I paid her parking tickets and electricity bills. I tried to get her to move in with me and my partners in Palm Springs, but she never showed up. I often suspected she had some form of drug addiction, and I even accused her of it, but she never admitted to anything.

Her issues only seemed to escalate. I finally reached a breaking point. "I love you so much," I said, "but I don't know how to help you." We had an in-depth conversation about what her next step should be. We made a deal: she would go live with her oldest son, who wanted her home with him more than anything. Sadly, that day never came.

On March 7, 2019, my nephew Craig called to tell me that Shari had been found dead where she was living in Rolla, Missouri.

The news just stunned me. I couldn't even process it. How was this possible? I had just talked to her the day before. I had no idea she was in such danger—all I could figure was that her despair, isolation, and depression had finally won out, and I

was so damn angry about it. I walked around in a daze, the loss so profound and the heartache so surreal, I felt absent from my own body. Everything happening around me felt foreign and far away.

In a random, cosmic chain of events, on the day I found out about Shari's death, I happened to be attending a personal-development event hosted by Mindvalley, which teemed with authors, life coaches, inspirational speakers, and spiritual teachers such as Marianne Williamson, Lisa Nichols, Jason Goldberg, Sarah Prout, and many more. Talk about being in the most profound place at the worst possible time! I stopped in hidden areas of the hotel lobby and just fell apart. Every part of me wanted to run straight back home.

But soon I found myself in a love bubble made up of this crazy-loving band of superheroes. No sooner did I walk into the lobby of the hotel than I was met by my friend Christina Hepburn. She held me tightly for what felt like forever. I sobbed. She knew, and so did everyone else. My mind flooded with messages. *You need this love right now. You need it to hold you up.* I knew I couldn't do anything for Shari in that moment. My younger brother Jimmy was handling all the details. I wouldn't be of any use to anyone in Missouri that day.

Before the event kicked off, I contacted Donnie to let him know about Shari.

"I assume she was on drugs," he said.

I was so angry about his assumption that I couldn't stay on the phone with him. Why would he jump to such a conclusion? Shari had congestive heart failure. A hospital had once sent her home with a heart vest that would shock her back to life if her heart stopped beating. She was only fifty-one years old—I figured her health problems were from stress and smoking.

But his words nagged at me. I knew she'd had issues with substance abuse in the past, but given my history as a serious drug addict, surely I would have known if Shari was struggling with a lethal addiction. There was no way I could have missed that. Finally, I broke down and contacted Jimmy, who lived near our parents outside of Carson City, Nevada.

"I just have to ask you, was Shari on drugs?"

"You really want to know?" he asked.

"Yes," I said, sort of lying.

"Yes, she was. Pain meds, but mostly meth."

I couldn't fucking believe it. This is just how manipulative, cunning, and powerful the disease of addiction is. For years and years, I'd heard Shari say, "Drugs are awful. Drugs have killed my friends. I don't do that shit, and I don't want that shit around me." And I believed her. I'm not someone who can be fooled—I can tell a tweaker from ten miles away. I've sponsored many guys who have come to me saying, "I'm not using. I'm not high. I don't do that stuff." And I could feel it, even over the phone. But not with Shari.

Jimmy had also been sending Shari financial support, and he kept her drug use a secret so Craig wouldn't find out. Jimmy told me he'd checked Shari into multiple drug treatment programs over the years, but she rarely stuck it out.

After Shari had agreed to go live with Craig, I called him to confirm that everything was set.

"She said she's not coming," he said. "She's not ready. Apparently, she has the flu right now, and she just needs some rest." She told him she loved him, they hung up, and she died sometime later.

"I'm not ready" is something addicts say when they're still stuck in the delusion that they can manage their addiction. Shari couldn't comprehend how to live without access to

oblivion, and she died as a result. What happened to her could easily have happened to me, but it didn't. It happened to my witness, my shield, my protector.

Little research has documented how child abuse affects the lives of the siblings of children who were made the scapegoat. My own deduction is that Shari—being my usual witness and only defender—felt unbearable guilt, and she suffered from being unable to help me. I was armed to the teeth with resistance and screamed for help, fighting for my life. She could do nothing. In some ways, she was more abused than I was. Rarely did I have a conversation with her in which she didn't apologize for what happened to me. She almost blamed herself.

Jimmy made all the arrangements for her memorial service, which was scheduled for ten in the morning on Tuesday, March 12, 2019, at the Saint Patrick Catholic Church in Rolla, Missouri. Jimmy didn't want any money from me; he insisted he would do it all on his own. But being the proud older brother, I sent him and my nephews as much money as my bank account would cough up, and we managed to cover the costs of Shari's cremation and memorial service.

At first, I had no intention of actually going—I couldn't stand the idea of facing my parents, whom I hadn't seen in about fourteen years. I resisted making any travel arrangements up until the afternoon before the ceremony, but I knew my sister would want me to be there for her boys. I flew into St. Louis the night before the service and drove a rental car more than a hundred miles to Rolla. Though I was going to support my brothers and nephews, there were moments I was consumed by thoughts of self-interest. Was I still hoping that, in the midst of a crisis, my parents would finally pour out the love I'd been craving all my life? I had

no expectations whatsoever, but I had grown accustomed to seeking their approval every time we came face-to-face.

My sponsor would say, "You keep going to this well, and no one's putting water in it. You can stop expecting it to happen."

What if they did? Would it change anything? Rarely, if ever, would I consider the possibility that I needed anything else from them. But this was not the time. Maybe I could just show up, be present, and get out as soon as possible.

The day of Shari's service, I stopped at a local gas station where I spent forty minutes in my car, doing deep, intentional breath work. Tapping into my breathing was about all I had left, aside from downing a bottle of whiskey, which would have been the worst idea ever. I was thankful that the breath work eliminated enough of the stress and anxiety that I could drive the rest of the way to the church.

When I walked into the church foyer, I saw my family gathered near the entrance to the sanctuary. Donnie had flown in from Southern California. He and I hadn't communicated much over the years. He'd had his own falling out with Jim before the transfer to Missouri, and he packed up his stuff and moved to Los Angeles. He married his wife, Janet, and they have a daughter, Stephanie, whom he adores. She is an athlete and an honor student. Every year, I have made it a point to buy as many Girl Scout cookies from her as I can. Donnie and I aren't that close, but we stay in touch, and I want to be supportive in any way I can.

My parents had flown in from Carson City, Nevada, where they had been living for eighteen years to be near Jim's son from his first marriage, Trevor, and Trevor's family. My mother and stepfather, now in their mid-seventies, looked like older, miniature versions of their formerly formidable selves. I opened my arms to embrace my mom, who sobbed softly.

Clearly, she was heartbroken. She looked so tiny and frail; her vulnerability streamed through me. I felt so much compassion for her in that moment, a familiar and yet unusual feeling. I didn't hang onto her for long—I cherished the moment and saw it for what it was.

Jim stuck out his hand, but instead of shaking it, I pulled him toward me and wrapped him in a big hug. I have no clue why I did that, but my true self will never turn away from a chance to love someone. I'm certain it caught him off guard, and by no means was it a remedy or even a mind-set of denial. But everyone was hurting, and we needed to be present for those boys.

"It's very nice to see you," I said, as I drew back and looked at him.

"It's nice to see you, too," said Jim. "I had to ask your mother who you were. I didn't recognize you."

"I bet! I mean, just look at me. Don't I look good?"

Everybody started laughing. My brothers and I started cracking jokes, the only way any of us knew to ease the tension and awkwardness of this unplanned reunion. My nephew Jake was the first to nudge me and say, "You know Shari's really pissed right now that she had to die to get us all together." That was all Shari ever wanted for our family—for her parents, her brothers, and her sons to know and love one another. She never gave up trying to pull from that well.

About thirty-five people we didn't know showed up as well, friends of Shari's who obviously cared about her. They were predominantly poor, down-home folks wrought with problems of their own. Several of them told me she was like a second mom to them and what a pistol she was, a force to be reckoned with.

On the plane ride from California to Missouri, I had texted Jimmy. "Do you think they're gonna want people to come up and say a few words?"

"Big brother, I was too afraid to ask you," he wrote back. "Please, I would love it so very much if you would come up and say something. I don't think I can do it."

I spent the rest of the flight preparing my message. I couldn't share any memories from childhood because those years were fraught with abuse and trauma. There were no cute little stories of us as kids. "Oh, Shari and I used to make mud pies when we were little." Those kinds of memories didn't exist for me. If there had been any moments like that, they were buried in the blur.

During the memorial service, the priest preached a dry, uninteresting sermon with such a lack of enthusiasm I could only assume he was in a hurry to get home to his television programs. When the time came for my eulogy, I walked toward the altar and took my place behind the lectern, but then something came over me. I decided not to stand behind it—I wanted to speak unobstructed. Feeling heavy and nervous, I wasn't sure how to stay present in my body. Through a surreal haze, I looked at my despondent parents sitting in the front row. I saw my brothers and nephews all staring into the abyss of this stunning sadness. I took a long, deep breath, and began.

"I want to tell you a story I love about a hummingbird, a tale from some African lore. It goes something like this. A giant forest has caught fire, and as the trees burn, the flames drive all of the elephants and lions and tigers out of the forest. They sit transfixed on the outskirts, overwhelmed by the blaze, all except for a little hummingbird, who flies back and forth from a stream. She takes one drop of water at a time from the stream and drops it on the fire.

"A lion and an elephant stare at her. 'What do you think you're doing? You're too small,' roared the lion. 'You can only carry one drop at a time,' cried the elephant. The other animals told her the fire was hopeless. Those who could carry much more water did nothing to help. No one had any hope that it would do any good. The hummingbird continued to fly back and forth, dropping small drops of water onto the flames. She stopped only for a moment, and in her exhaustion and determination—"

I paused for a brief moment to allow everyone to sit in the stillness of the story. My expression deep and sincere, I choked back tears.

"The hummingbird replied, 'I'm doing the best that I can.'"

I took a few seconds to look out the windows, trying to stop my tears. I gathered myself together and cleared my throat.

"I believe that's what my sister was doing; she was doing the best she could. I read a book by Marianne Williamson called *A Return to Love*. One of her most famous quotes says, 'Our deepest fear is not that we are inadequate. Our deepest fear is that we are powerful beyond measure. It is our light, not our darkness, that most frightens us.' Another part says, 'We are all meant to shine, as children do. We were born to make manifest the glory of God that is within us. It's not just in some of us; it's in everyone. And as we let our own light shine, we unconsciously give other people permission to do the same.'[4]

"When I read that part, I so wanted to call bullshit—sorry, I know I'm in church, and I love God, but I'm angry. I believed

4 Marianne Williamson, *A Return to Love: Reflections on the Principles of "A Course in Miracles"* (New York: HarperPerennial, 1996), 190–191.

in this idea. I shined so bright—I'd say, 'Look at me, Shari! Look at me go.' I shined so bright I could light a city block. My sister cheered from the sidelines. All she did was brag about how great I was. She saw what was possible, but it didn't save her.

"You see, I assumed Shari wasn't shining—she was lost in pain and despair. What I didn't understand was that she was shining her light in her own way. She often called me when she found herself in a predicament, and sometimes I got so mad at her. But now I'm grateful. I'm grateful she trusted me enough to ask me for help. Who am I to think she wasn't shining brightly? The friends gathered here, and her family who loved her, all thought her shine was bright and beautiful, just as it was."

Though I felt overwhelmed by emotion, I put power into this message—I believed Shari was doing the best she could and that had to be enough.

"There's a saying inspired by 'A Course in Miracles' that says, 'Every decision is a choice between a grievance and a miracle.' You're supposed to pray, 'Today, I release all grievances. Today, I choose the miracle.' But this particular day, I choose the grievance. I choose to grieve the painful heartache that is the miracle of my sister's bright light. All of our memories of her, her influence on our lives, are her drops of water from the stream. She was doing the best she could. She was my North Star—she meant everything to me."

I suddenly grabbed a country preacher twang from my voice box and said, "If you want to throw a bucket of water on that burning forest, then we must forgive each other, forgive ourselves, forgive all of it, completely and fully! We can give Shari the gift of a well-tended fire, no longer burning out of control. She would love that."

I paused. I could feel the tension in the chapel. It was now or never. I looked directly at my stepfather, the man I had despised for most of my life, the man who would never hear my requests for love, the man who could never see my wholeness. He was staring in a catatonic daze, but I knew he could hear me.

In a low but serious voice, I said, "Today, I relinquish all grievances. Today, I choose the miracle. I love you, Shari."

I gazed gently at my parents, trying to look at my mother as much as I could without her noticing. I had no intention of inflicting a sense of guilt or shame on them. I was trying to be present and see this moment for what it was—not something fluffy and airy but an opportunity for closure to release any unfinished business lingering within me. I believe that deep down inside of every individual is our core emotion, which is love, plain and simple. I knew that somewhere in their souls, my parents heard me. I wanted resolution not just for me but for Shari. I wanted to be a good custodian of my sister's memory.

When I left the altar, I was still in this surreal plane of existence. I sat down in the pew next to my family, and I felt a sort of upwelling in my spine, as if every vertebra shifted upright. I closed my eyes and felt for the first time in my life that I was no longer slightly hunched over, bracing myself against the onslaught of life. Since childhood, so much unresolved shame and darkness had rounded my shoulders, but after delivering Shari's eulogy, my posture straightened. I felt lighter, as if my spirit had whispered, "Sit up. Be present. Feel the relief of this moment."

Staring at the bland birch walls of the church, I remembered one of the prayer services in the chapel at Santa Rita, when the sister gripped my hand. "Don't bow down," she had

whispered. "Look up! You never know what God has in store for you, baby. So, look up. Always look up."

Then, Jimmy wrapped his arm around my shoulder to thank me, and I snapped out of it. I don't know whether I felt utter and total forgiveness steeped in love and compassion, but maybe total forgiveness isn't even necessary. Maybe there's something more powerful than forgiveness. What if I just accepted them right where they were in the moment? It's what I always wanted from them myself. At least I had found resolution, a completion to the story. I knew to my core that I no longer needed to run to a dry well for love that wasn't there. I didn't need to find their love—I could be the well itself.

When the service ended, my mom said, "That was just so beautiful. Thank you for that."

I smiled, though the moment between us felt awkward.

Jim stood up. "What you said up there really got me. As soon as you started talking about the hummingbird, it hit me hard." Tears filled his eyes. I could see this man had been broken from the inside out, worn down by the day. The entire service hadn't lasted more than an hour, but it had felt like four. "And when you said she was doing the best she could, I just pictured her as that six-year-old—" and at the same time, we both said, "trying to count pennies."

Each of my siblings had a story our parents told that we could never live down. For Shari, it was the time she was six years old and learning to count. Jim used to say, "She was so dumb, we'd put a nickel and a penny together and ask her to add them up. And if one and five make six, she'd say it made two." Shari was counting the number of coins, but that's how my parents twisted things. They placed a label on this little girl who was powerful beyond measure. She carried the weight of that story all her life, too afraid to become

someone brilliant. She would never believe you if you told her how magical she was, because from the beginning she was taught she was not. After all, she couldn't even add a few pennies.

Despite this memory, it was strange how much compassion I felt for Jim, a love maybe not born of forgiveness but manifested because I needed to move on.

We went out to eat at a buffet; we chatted a little bit, laughed, and cried. We told stories about Shari. We talked about food, grasping at points in common that would nurture this tenuous bond. In the buffet line, I said, "Look, Mom, there's macaroni and cheese."

"Ugh, I hate it," she said.

"What are you talking about?" I turned to wink at Jim. "I happen to think macaroni and cheese with hot dogs is the best dish ever."

Mom and Jim started cracking up—macaroni and cheese with sliced hot dogs was a dish he used to make, a big pot of it for the whole family. It was amazing, the most delicious thing you ever ate, if you were five years old and starving.

He beamed at me. "I bet you put your eggs on hash browns, too. You see, I learned you guys some good stuff."

I smiled, content to let this exchange be what it was, a moment of togetherness for Shari's sake, not that we had magically transformed into a happy family.

I'd agreed to hang out for a little while, but I couldn't stand it for long. At one point, I took Shari's son Craig outside. "Listen, I don't think you understand how difficult it is for me to be with my parents. I came here because I needed to be here for you and the boys and for Jimmy. Shari needs us to take care of each other. I want to stay connected. I want us to have a life together."

In the midst of his grief, Craig nodded and gave me a reluctant goodbye. He was so strong on every front, but this was too much. His mother had meant everything to him.

My family and I parted company later that afternoon, and I headed straight for the airport. My whole being felt electrified, lighter, clean. I was grateful that I'd been able to show up as my authentic self. Shari had been my shield, but now that shield had transformed into a beautiful bond that reconnected me to my brothers and my nephews. I drove to the airport immersed in an ocean of sadness, barely able to see through my tears. Losing my sister is a deep wound no spiritual awakening can ever fully heal. I miss her every day.

Despite how badly Jim abused me, despite what Norman did to me, and despite how much I tried to destroy myself, I know the way to gratitude. I have found the map to be filled with markers, road signs, and detours. The directions are seldom crystal clear. The key to understanding the route is surrender. In letting go of everything I think I know, I find this wonderful dance of poignant beauty, filled with all the color and emotion of life.

In the midst of this dance, I'm surrounded by opportunities to find understanding, compassion, and joy. I don't dare deny anger or anxious fear. I don't look away from suffering. I don't avoid the visceral pain that teaches empathy. I get to fully experience all of it—the love, sadness, kindness, and frustration that comes with the waking hours I've been given. I'm not striving for the elusive path to some healed place or the idea of being in some cosmic alignment with my true purpose. I believe I am there already. If we look closely enough, we find out we are right where we belong. It doesn't mean I don't have more work to do or that I don't want to grow and expand. It just means that what I think is missing has yet to be uncovered.

I realize now more than ever that my job is to be who I am in this moment. I continue to try my best to be an instrument of kindness and to shine a light. To do so, I must remain open and grounded in my truth. I was given a second chance, and I took it, but I did nothing on my own. I stand on the shoulders of every person I have ever met, everyone who rejected me, and everyone who saved me.

With these well-worn hiking boots on my feet and my pack on my back, I'm living a life beyond my wildest dreams. I have my family all around me. I'm still traveling the world on one adventure after another. But I have only just begun to discover how vast and beautiful the world we live in truly is.

The one thing I know for sure—and nothing else—is that we are all messengers, and we deliver our message to the world by the love we convey, the deeds we do, and the pain we endure. I read somewhere that we are all either expressing love or requesting love. From that understanding, we can find true compassion for each other.

One truth remains—love is all that matters. Only love is real.

Acknowledgements

There are many, many people who helped make this book happen. You know who you are, and I cannot wait to stand face-to-face, hold you in my arms, and thank you personally.

First of all, a huge thanks to everyone who preordered a copy of the book during my Publishizer campaign, especially to the "Healers," Luke Adams, Angela Avery, Jeff Coulter, Keith Cunningham, Barry Layfer, Robert Martin, Jaime McElmon, Robert McNamara, Steven McNeil, Terry Moore, Brien O'Brien, Hal Paul, Hugh Walker, Ric West, Roni Westray, and Alicia White, and the "Spirit Guides," Carl Borey, Arnold Dito, Meredith Karns, and William Pfleghardt. Without your support, this book might never have made it to print.

To JuLee Brand and her team at W. Brand Publishing—you showed up in perfect timing and turned out to be the partner we had been praying for. Thank you for your enthusiasm, creativity, and dedication to this work.

To Todd and Carl (my Corey), I have never been loved this much. Without you, my life would be so different. Thank you for listening to me as I jumped up and down with excitement and for suffering through every turn of this crazy roller-coaster ride. To Kurt, you have given me the keys to stay grateful and embody the messenger within me. To Judge Hamilton and Bobby Love, you believed in me before I knew who I could be.

To friends far and wide who stuck by me even as I melted down, the ones who said, "Fuck them! You have work to do. We're waiting." Here I am.

To Florence Welch, thank you for seeing me. Thank you for inspiring me to write from my heart and to leave nothing out.

To my sister Sonia, thank you for cheering me on, for giving me courage, for bringing my life to my father before he passed away. You will always be in my heart. Rest in your courage and strength.

To Maggie, who kept me grounded and stood in line for hours at every show, you're the best friend I never imagined.

To Professor Matthew Knip, thank you for your instructive and adamant truth about queer and gay history, your ability to stand up and educate, and most importantly for being my friend.

To Howie for everything you have done for me thank you for being there.

To all the sex workers who stand by while the world shames you, and you do the work anyway, you are why this book was written. To my clients who are my family, you mean the world to me. No matter why you chose to heal, to be brave, to love sex without shame, and to just be who you are, this book is yours as well.

There have been many people responsible for my story not ending in a dark alley or a prison cell. If you are in recovery and sharing your story in any form, you are saving lives, and you have impacted mine. You have healed me.

Finally, I couldn't imagine spending years trying to write this book in a dark hotel room all on my own. When the weight of this journey overwhelmed me, I faced two choices: I could just drop it altogether, let the past be the past, and forget about it. Or I could ask for help. Finding Heather was just the miracle I needed.

To Heather Ebert, the archaeologist of my story: There were times I wanted to stop seeing the truth and just keep telling the stories I told to protect myself. There were times I couldn't even breathe. With compassion, precision, and patience, you continued to believe in this story. You never once said, "This isn't working." You found all of the dark corners, facts that mattered, and hidden truths I never wanted to face that were coloring my perception. With grace and some sort of cosmic magic, you put this book in my hands and said, "This is important. This is powerful. This matters. I can help you. We do this until it's done, and we do it together." One of the most important gifts you have given me is freedom to own my story, to be the author of my message. My North Star, thank you.

About the Author

David P. Wichman is an author, speaker, sexual healer, and entrepreneur passionate about his message. He is respected and well-known all over the world to those who seek to renew themselves and explore ways to live a fulfilling life free of stigma, shame, and fear around sex, love, and intimacy.

Raised in Fremont, California, David survived a childhood marked by severe neglect and physical, emotional, and sexual abuse. The trauma of his early life led him into years of homelessness, alcoholism, and drug addiction. After decades of struggle and rehabilitation failures, he finally obtained freedom from his addiction in 2005. He remains an active member of New Thought and recovery movements to this day.

In 2006, when David began his journey into sex work, unbeknownst to him he found his calling. While working with sometimes marginalized men, such as seniors, the disabled, and those with severe intimacy issues, he discovered the profound transformational power that sex work creates for both client and provider.

In 2009, David founded his travel-companion company, the Male Adventure, through which he has accompanied clients on life-changing adventures to all seven continents. His trips have featured safaris in the Serengeti, bungee jumping in New Zealand, swimming with humpback whales in Tonga, treks to mountain gorillas in Uganda, and much more. He believes his connection to conservation, wildlife, and different

cultures has given him a more intuitive ability to respond to the human condition.

He is an activist, vocal ally, and grateful member of the LGBTQI2 community and stays connected to current and emerging issues that dominate marginalized communities. He is a passionate fundraiser for HIV- and AIDS-related causes and other nonprofits supporting other-abled persons and benefiting animal rescues.

In 2011, David created and began facilitating a workshop called "Sex, Love, and Intimacy: Writing Your Way to New Relationships" for recovery conferences and retreats. Groups have used his highly sought-after writing workshop in Los Angeles, New York, Atlanta, the San Francisco Bay Area, and Sydney, Australia, with great success.

In 2016, David and his partners, Carl and Todd, founded Heal-VR, a software development company that merges ancient spiritual principles and meditation techniques with modern virtual reality technology. Heal-VR creates content that offers users a deeper and more profound meditative experience.

Undergirding all of David's personal and professional efforts has been a deep and abiding mystical spirituality. He is currently a student of "A Course in Miracles" and utilizes New Thought practices, such as life visioning, creative visualization, and meditation. While he has studied the works of many modern healers, his deeper healing in recovery has been under the guidance of his spiritual mentor, T. J. Woodward. David's spiritual practices have brought him an overwhelming sense of gratitude and an unending wealth of forgiveness and joy on his journey to true wholeness.

David lives with his partners and their three dogs in the Coachella Valley area of California.

About the Coauthor

Heather Ebert is a professional writer based near Nashville, Tennessee. She has more than fifteen years' experience in print and digital publishing and has written for a variety of publications. Heather specializes in memoir, fiction, and narrative nonfiction, helping nonwriters tell their stories with power and beauty. She has written nine other books to date. One of her recently published books is *Sole Survivor: The inspiring true story of coming face-to-face with the infamous Railroad Killer* by Holly K. Dunn with Heather Ebert (Diversion Books, 2017). Learn more at heatherebert.com.

CPSIA information can be obtained
at www.ICGtesting.com
Printed in the USA
LVHW052312020320
648719LV00004B/415

9 781950 385133